W9-CPE-910

Bringing a Product to Market From Your Home

With $500 and an Idea
YOU CAN MAKE MILLIONS

First Edition

Written by Gary R. Bronga

Published in the United States by the
Clipeze Worldwide Inc.

Published by:
Clipeze Worldwide Inc.
P.O. BOX 373
Mims, Florida 32754-0373
http://www.clipeze.com

Written by: Gary R. Bronga
Editing: Lou Belcher

Cover design and Illustration: Gary R. Bronga

Library of Congress Control Number: 2009912992

10 9 8 7 6 5 4 3 2 1

Published in the United States of American
First Printing 2010

ISBN: 0615339972

Soft Cover 978-0-615-33997-9
E-book 978-0-615-34721-9

Dedicated to my wife of 35 years, Sandy. She is the hardest working and most generous person I have ever met. Her unconditional support in good times and in bad times made our business and this book possible.

Genius is one percent inspiration and ninety-nine percent perspiration. - Thomas Jefferson

Table of Contents

About the Author

This book is based on my first-hand, been-there-done-that experiences. Many people have many great ideas. They just don't act on them. You can do it differently.

I worked in the aerospace industry at Cape Canaveral, Florida, for 21 years. Wearing identification badges had always been a part of my working wardrobe. A large aerospace company handed out a lapel pin for a promotion in the spring of 1995. Just by chance, I pinned my company identification badge to the lapel pin.

An idea for a better way to wear my identification badge came to me. For several days, I made many drawings and came up with the idea to place a "bar" at the bottom of a lapel pin to accommodate the common bulldog metal clip on identification badges. This enabled me to make badge holders with custom logos for companies or associations and to create many fun designs that would make wearing badges more personal and enjoyable.

This was the start of my journey.

This book is intended to streamline your own process of taking a product from an idea to reality. Potentially it will expedite the process of putting money into your pocket.

I started with my computer and only $500.00. Originally, I had enough rejection letters to wallpaper my home office. Most of the people and companies that rejected me then call me now.

To date, we have sold over 3-million CLIPEZE badge holders. They have been sold in over 1,100 uniform stores and 20 catalogs around the world.

One sales representative even placed it on the television show *ER* (the number one rated show in America at the time).

We are currently concentrating on penetrating other markets, making gains on Internet sales, and leveraging my ideas into other new products.

I often consult with entrepreneurs to help them attain their dreams to bring new products to market from their homes. I started CLIPEZE in the smallest bedroom of my home, moved to a larger bedroom, then finally to over 3,000-square feet of commercial office space.

I left my aerospace job and the need to wear my own identification badge for a chance to be my own boss, make my own decisions, and create my own future.

I believe that anyone can do what I did with his or her own product.

You can contact me directly at:

Gary R. Bronga, President
Clipeze Worldwide Inc.
P.O. Box 373
Mims, Florida 32754 321-264-7599
admin@clipeze.com

Warning-Disclaimer

This book is designed to provide information on bringing a new product to market from your home. It is sold with the understanding that the publisher and author are not engaged in rendering legal, accounting or other professional services. If legal or other expert assistance is required, the services of a competent professional should be sought. It is not the purpose of this book to reprint all the information that is available to persons looking to bring a product to market from their homes, but instead to complement, amplify and supplement other texts. You are urged to read all the available material, learn as much as possible about this subject and tailor the information to your individual needs. For more information, see the many resources in the back of this book.

Bringing a product to market from your home is not a get-rich-quick scheme. Anyone who decides to bring a product or service to market must expect to invest a lot of time and effort into it. Every effort has been made to make this book as complete and as accurate as possible. However, there may be mistakes, both typographical and in content. Therefore, this text should be used only as a general guide and not as the ultimate source for bringing a product to market from your home.

Furthermore, this book contains information that is current only up to the printing date. The purpose of this manual is to educate and entertain. The author and Clipeze Worldwide Inc. shall have neither liability nor responsibility to any person or entity with respect to any loss or damage caused, or alleged to have been caused, directly or indirectly, by the information contained in this book.

Foreword

As the president of the National Nurses in Business Association (NNBA), I have interacted with entrepreneurs for the past ten years helping them build their businesses.

Many of them had great ideas and were interested in bringing their products to market. I have done a lot of research looking for information on successfully bringing a product to market. I found many books and people offering services to inventors. Additional investigation often revealed that the people who wrote the books never actually brought a product to market. Also, the people who offered services to inventors often did not have any real-world experience and charged unreasonable fees.

With this book, all that has changed. Gary Bronga has the real-world knowledge needed to bring a product to market from your home and make a profit. He presents it in this book, *Bringing Your Product to Market from Your Home*, in simple, understandable language.

Gary was the first to tell me that not all great ideas make money. He told me about inexpensive testing (testing you do yourself) to see if your product will sell. Gary told me that a patent isn't always necessary and why. He shares all this information and more with you in his book.

This book offers the information you need to successfully bring your product to market from your home and to build a profitable business.

Patricia Bemis, RN CEN
President
National Nurses in Business Association, Inc.
PO Box 561081Rockledge, FL 32956 (321) 633-4610 www.nnba.net
bemis@nnba.net

Chapter 1

Generating a Unique Product Idea

Think about the times you have said something like, "Why hasn't someone invented a product that would do _____?"

That question can be the beginning of a unique product. You have probably had those thoughts and let them go without capturing them.

Write down your ideas for products the next time you notice them surfacing in your thoughts. Capture an idea without judging it and regardless of how incomplete it is in your mind. It can be developed later if you decide you want to take it to the next level.

Day-to-day chores or problems bring opportunities for new products. Many new products, such as the Weed Eater®, were created to make a chore much easier or to save time doing an unpleasant but necessary task.

We all have too little time in the busy world we live in. Some of the most successful products save us time. If your product idea makes life easier, it may have potential. I say too often, "They can put a man on the moon but can't make a coffee pot that doesn't spill when you pour from it." Some of the best products come from very simple ideas.

Go to the US Patent and Trademark Office web site if you think you have no product ideas of your own. The web address is http://www.uspto.gov/. This web site can provide ideas regarding the competition you may encounter.

In addition, the US Patent and Trademark Office web site has thousands of patents and many can be leased from the patent owner for a percentage or royalty.

Look at expired patents, too. Patents generally only last 17 to 20 years. Anyone can produce a product that has an expired patent.

Sometimes an old idea is much more valuable when made from today's materials. You may be able to file a new patent on an old idea by improving it in some way.

Leverage your first idea into additional products as you develop your business. A unique design in one form can be expanded and manufactured in other forms. This will allow you to create an entire product line from a single idea or group of ideas.

It is important for your idea to serve a niche in the market. The smaller the niche the better, because a small niche allows you to concentrate on that market and that market only. Later, you may migrate into new niches as a way to expand your business.

My idea began one day on my job in 1995. I was employed at Cape Canaveral Air Force Station near the Kennedy Space Center in Central Florida. During a discussion with some co-workers the subject centered on our mutual dislike for wearing mandatory company identification badges. Just by chance a man from another company came by and gave us a lapel pin that his company was handing out for a promotion.

After everyone left, I happened to attach my ID badge to the lapel pin by attaching the little alligator clip to the bottom of the pin. That's when the idea hit me. I thought if I just put a little cutout at the bottom of a lapel pin, it could accommodate the alligator clip attached to any and all ID badges.

I set out to design a lapel pin with a cut-out space and a bar at the bottom. I wanted to make it possible to create custom designs from logos of corporations or to make stock pins with logos from several industries to keep on hand so they could be sold individually. It took me weeks to prefect the design.

I drew designs on pieces of paper for many days. At night, I would wake up with another idea as to how it would look. I got to the point that I kept a pen and paper on my nightstand to write down ideas that came to me in the middle of the night. This is something I still do today, however, I have modernized a bit and now use a digital recorder.

Good ideas keep you awake at night. I would go so far as to state that if you do not stay awake night after night, you might not be passionate enough to pursue your idea.

Most ideas come to people on their day job. Many come while addressing problems that cannot be solved. Other ideas come to people while spending time working on a hobby.

Your idea does not have to involve rocket science. You do not have to invent a new super computer. A simple idea is often best. An idea that inspires others to say, "Why didn't I think of that?" can make millions of dollars.

Chapter 2

What To Do with Your Idea

You need to find out if someone else already has a patent on the product you are thinking of developing. You do not want to infringe on an existing patent. Go to the US Patent and Trademark Office web site at http://www.uspto.gov. Click on the word Patents and conduct a simple patent search.

The directions for a search are found on the home page. A more complete and extensive search may be necessary at a later date to make sure that you are not infringing on some other party's patent if you decide a patent is needed for your product.

If someone already has a patent on your idea, contact him or her. Perhaps you can market the idea in exchange for a royalty or buy the patent outright from them. There are many great ideas that are patented but never brought to market. Sometimes the patent owner becomes ill or they just like the idea of the patent process but don't like marketing or sales. Or perhaps they tried and gave up on the idea. There are about as many reasons why a patent never becomes a product, as there are patents.

We will talk more about patents later in the book. For now, you need to evaluate your product to see if it is commercially viable to bring to the marketplace.

Draw your idea on paper as best as you can. Talk to your relatives and friends about your idea. Identify the industry(s) or niche that your invention should be marketed to. Start reading publications about that industry.

Go to a local inventor club meeting. Read inventor magazines. The United Inventors Association's website at http://www.uiausa.org is a great resource with a link to find local inventor clubs. Inventor clubs are made up of people just like you. They are looking to invent a new product or have already done so.

Do not confuse inventor clubs with inventor marketing companies. Inventor marketing or development companies are for profit and are discussed later in this book.

Making a Prototype of a Product

A prototype is needed to evaluate your product. It is also needed to lease or sell your product outright to a company.

Draw many versions of your idea as best as you can. Modify your drawings as your ideas become clearer to you. It is not necessary to be an artist to make rough sketches of your idea.

There are many places to find someone to make a prototype for you. One of the best places is an inventor club. You can use the link mentioned above to find the one closest to you. You can search for them on the web. Also, many advertise in or have announcements in local newspapers giving meeting places and times. Many of the members of these clubs have done or are doing exactly what you are trying to accomplish.

Some clubs invite guest speakers to attend. These speakers are often patent attorneys, design engineers, prototype makers, creative writers, and others who you can find to be very helpful. It is also a chance to see unique products and hear success stories of others. Going to a club is usually the least expensive way to get information about a prototype maker.

Another place that is often overlooked is a nearby community college or university. Call the department that best fits your product and see if they may be interested in making a prototype for you. Set up an appointment with them. Many community colleges have entrepreneur programs and host or sponsor inventor club meetings.

Many times, professors will use your product prototype as a project for student course credit. Sometimes, working with a school can lead to gaining other assistance later, such as marketing assistance from the business school or graphic design/web site development. In some cases, schools have literally become partners with local entrepreneurs.

Visit local businesses that manufacture products similar to your product. For example, if your product requires a plastic mold or injection molding, visit a local manufacturer that does this process and ask them for suggestions. Even if they cannot make a prototype for you, they may know someone in their industry who can.

As I write this book, the web search engine Google at: www.google.com, has over 4 million results for "prototype manufacturer". It lists all kinds of prototype manufacturers from plastics to electrical and everything in between.

Also, the local library has several directories of manufacturers. Dunn and Bradstreet is one of the most popular of these directories.

In my case, I asked friends and relatives and was told of a local manufacturing company that supplied awards and die-struck medallions to several companies where I worked. It was located within a few miles of my home.

One afternoon, I stopped by there and showed them my drawings. The man who owned the company said that they could not make the product, but he had a number in his files of a company that could. This company manufactured enamel lapel pins.

I called the company. All I needed to do was send the artwork and they would give me a price. We worked on the design and colors for a week or so, and I contracted to have 200 of my product manufactured.

The company was located in the US, however, I found out later they had them manufactured in Asia. I paid more for the items, but I learned a lot about design and other details about the manufacturing of my products.

After you receive a working prototype, test the product with family and friends. Test the product for safety, durability, and reliability. You may need to test your product made from different materials, such as metal vs. plastic.

At this point, you need to evaluate production and packaging costs as well. Again, I suggest making a prototype as close to home as possible so you can participate in any changes or improvements.

Many times, it is necessary to create several prototypes until you are satisfied with your new product.

Let me give you a hint about color of your products. If your product is to be produced in different colors, I have found a way to predict next year's hot colors. Go to a large department store and view the women's clothes from a distance. One or two colors will always pop out at you. These clothes designers test, study and spend large sums of money to predict the next popular colors.

Finding a Manufacturer for Your Product

The type and make up of your product many times dictates how and where your product should be manufactured.

In the beginning, I recommend having your product manufactured as close to home as you can. This way, you can continue to evaluate it and make modifications if necessary. You also have a chance to witness the manufacturing process so you become an expert on how your product should be produced.

The cost of manufacturing close to home probably will be higher, but your overhead is low, being a home-based business. At a later date when sales grow, you may choose to have your product made in Asia or some other overseas markets to hold down costs.

I suggest moving into overseas manufacturing slowly. Perhaps have some trial orders manufactured overseas while keeping your local manufacturer.

I recommend that you use more than one manufacturer. I say this because you never know when a manufacturer could change personnel or have quality issues or even go out of business. If you have more than one manufacturer, you can shift production and avoid a long delay in fulfilling your orders.

I learned this the hard way. I was manufacturing with only one company and one day the person with whom I'd been working left the company. The new person was not qualified or helpful. Orders started arriving late, artwork was misinterpreted, and I started to see quality issues. I had to scramble to find a new manufacturer and start over building a relationship. Today, we always have three manufacturers and divide up the orders accordingly.

You find manufacturers in the same way you found a prototype maker. Use all your resources, such as local inventor clubs, colleges and universities, and local businesses. Look on labels of other products made of similar construction in stores. Use the business directories to find manufacturers.

The web site www.globalsources.com is great for finding manufacturers in Asia. It is a free site to join. You can search for manufacturers or you can put out requests for product manufacturers to give you a quote. Describe your product and list a category and the companies will contact you by e-mail.

I do have a word of caution when choosing an Asian manufacturer. Move slowly. Place small "trial orders" with them. Make sure they understand that your business is an ongoing enterprise and you may order with them for years if all works out. They give better prices and better quality for orders with reorder possibilities versus a one-time order. Negotiate your price with these companies.

Check to see what companies they currently manufacture for or have manufactured for in the past. Check their web sites. Inquire if they attend any trade show in the US. If they do, perhaps they may give you a free pass to attend.

It takes time to build trust between your company and an Asian manufacturer. Over time, you will become friends and e-mail pals. My manufacturer expresses concern for us when they see the news about a hurricane in our area, and we about typhoons in theirs.

With the difference in time zones and the international date differences, communications with Asian companies is like communicating with a night shift. Send e-mail in the afternoon and have an answer the next morning.

Payment is often done not only by bank transfer but also by sending a business check as they have their own check-clearing houses.
With today's technology, the world has become a small place. Air shipments only take a few days.

I remember one request for samples from an Asian manufacturer arrived at my door before other samples I had requested from a nearby state.

Nearly all companies in Asia have good shipping rates with several carriers. Depending on the size and weight of your products, you may find it to your advantage to set up your own accounts with air carriers, such as DHL, FedEx and UPS. If you will ship your product in containers, contact some of your local freight forwarders to see if they can beat the shipping price the Asian manufacturer quotes you.

It is a small world indeed. On several occasions, we have had shipments leave Hong Kong and arrive at our warehouse in three days. Most overseas manufacturers are masters at manufacturing and duplicating your product, but they are very weak as innovators.

It is very difficult to get them to change, modify or improve a product. Be prepared to get a new prototype if you want to make substantial changes to your product.

Chapter 3

Protecting Your Idea

There are three types of intellectual properties: trademarks, patents, and copyrights.

I suggest that when you decide to spend money on a prototype, it is time to file a provisional application with the US Patent and Trademark Office.

Provisional Application

A provisional application filed with the patent office is a great way to record the date you first thought of your idea. This simple form may give you some recourse if someone you disclosed your idea to claims your idea as their own. Also, it may afford you some protection if someone else independently thinks of your idea at a later date.

A provisional application only requires a basic description and simple drawings of your invention and offers you a way to date the conception of your product.

In Appendix 1 I have provided the web site address and text taken directly from the US Patent Office about the provisional application.

Later, if you decide to file a non-provisional patent (regular patent) you may get the benefit of the earlier date you filed on your provisional patent.

The filling fee, as this book is being written, is $110.00. As provisional patent fees change from time to time, you should check fees just before you file the application. You may fill out a Provisional Patent Application online. The web site provides a template cover sheet for your use.

Nondisclosure Agreement

I also recommend using a nondisclosure agreement and have a potential prototype maker sign the form before you talk to them about producing the prototype.

A nondisclosure agreement is a legal contract that prevents individuals from disclosing secret or confidential information about your idea or product.

There are many free, non-disclosure forms on the web. Simply type "nondisclosure agreement forms" into Google or other search engines. You can also find one at www.nolo.com which is available for a small fee.

You can sue for damages if a person fails to comply with the non-discloser agreement.

Download a copy of the form and save it on your computer. You can use it over and over by just changing the dates and names of the individuals and printing it out for them to sign.

You should have all persons with whom you discuss your product and all people who work on your product sign the statement, including any employees you may hire.

Ask for and check references on people and companies with whom you seek to do business. It is a good idea to keep written records of individuals with whom you have talked about your product with the date the discussion took place. A good way to do this is to follow up each phone conversation with an e-mail summarizing what was said.

Chapter 4

Protecting Your Product

Once you have tested your new prototype and have perfected the product, you need to determine whether or not you need to file a Non-Provisional Patent Application.

A patent is a grant from a government that gives an inventor the right to exclude others from making, using, selling, importing, or offering an invention for sale for a fixed period of time.

A misconception about a patent is that some believe that if they get a patent they will become rich and famous. This is not the case. If your invention is not developed, leased or purchased commercially, it may become worthless.

A patent provides offensive rights, but it is not a guarantee against having your product copied. A patent holder must sue or threaten to sue any party that infringes. This can be very expensive. You have one year from the first commercial sale to patent your product. Once you are in production and have tested your product, you will need to make the decision to patent or not.

The book *Patent it Yourself* by David Pressman can help determine your need for a patent, trademark, or copyright and helps you understand what is involved with filing a patent and performing patent searches.

I highly recommend this book. You will find information about it in the Resources section in the last chapter of this book. Patent attorneys are very expensive, so you may consider patenting your product yourself. *Patent It Yourself* is published by Nolo Publishing Co. It explains the three types of patents: design, utility, and plant, and which may be the best, if any, for you and your product.

Consider if your idea even needs some form of protection or should you just start to market it. Many people go to the expense of patenting their product only to improve the product a short time later, rendering the original patent virtually useless.

The US Patent and Trademark Office only has

about 6,000 examiners. They receive over 1,000 submissions a day and have an estimated backlog of about 750,000 applications. This has complicated the situation for anyone applying for a patent. A company can do a search and not find any very similar invention(s) and complete the patent process only to find later, sometimes years later, that another company actually holds the patent on their item. This is because the patent office bases the order in which they receive patent applications as the criteria for awarding patents when there is a dispute between similar items.

Thousands of products in the past have been successful without patent protection. We live in a rip-off or knock-off society, and most successful products will be copied at a later date, regardless of whether or not they have patent protection.

Plan your marketing for being copied. Think about what you will do if/when your product is copied. Think of improvements or new designs ahead of time and have them ready to move to market.

Even if you receive a patent, you will need money to defend it in court if another party infringes.

Some companies actually are in the business of ripping off successful products. Often they are owned by or partially owned by lawyers, which enables them to have an unfair advantage with court costs.

These companies have also been known to put a percentage of funds aside for royalties or settlements if they are ever challenged for infringement. It appears that these companies feel they can always settle a case with a patent holder with an offer of back royalties.

Trademarks

Trademarks, copyrights and patents all differ. A copyright protects an original artistic or literary work; a patent protects an invention.

A trademark is a brand name. It is any word or symbol that is consistently attached to or forms part of a product to identify and distinguish it from others in the marketplace.

You need a trademark for your product and/or your business name. This is a great asset to your company. You can search trademarks on the US Patent and Trademark Office web site and register your trademark.

Go to:
http://www.uspto.gov/web/offices/tac/doc/basic/
to read the booklet *Basic Facts About Trademarks*

Domain Name

A domain name is the name or address of your web site, like ours www.clipeze.com. It's good to use the name of the product in your domain name. Search for the availability of the domain name you have chosen for your product. You can search for web site names by going to the web site of domain name companies, such as Go Daddy or Network Solutions at:
https://www.godaddy.com/gdshop/registrar/search.
http://www.networksolutions.com/whois/index.jsp

While the domain is available, it is advisable to buy it. You don't want someone else to buy that name before you do. It costs less than ten dollars to get the domain name for a year. You can renew it for several years later after you have been in business for some time.

Company Logo

A logo is very important to a business. You can obtain royalty-free clip art from web sites, such as www.clipart.com to help you create a company logo. Try to keep it simple and descriptive of your product. It is advisable to make your logo in one color to save on printing costs. Remember your logo will be on stationary, business cards, etc.

It can cost a lot of money to have a company logo created by a graphic arts company. You often can have a great logo made inexpensively by some other sources, such as a college/college student or a university graphics department.

Remember, the best protection you can have for a product is to sell the *most products the fastest* in a specific market. Doing this can make your product name synonymous with the product line. In this way, you can capture the highest market share in your industry or marketplace.

Think of products like Xerox® copiers or Scotch Tape®. They own the market share and always will unless they make a drastic error, because they were the first to market and they sold the most products the fastest. You hear many people say, "Let me make a Xerox of this paper," or, "Pass the Scotch Tape." These names have become synonymous with the product.

Invention or Invention marketing companies

Beware of invention marketing companies that advertise on TV or in inventor magazines. Most of these can result in a waste of large amounts of money. There may be some good companies that can help you evaluate your ideas and help you market them, but I have not heard of any.

Most are only after an upfront fee —followed by another fee and another fee. All they will do is submit your ideas to companies that you can submit to yourself for the price of a postage stamp and a little time spent on research.

Always ask for references from these marketing companies before signing up to do business with them. If all you get are excuses as to why they cannot furnish references walk away.

They do not guarantee anything except to take your money. Only do business with companies that will furnish references that you can check.

Be aware that after you file for a patent, you will most likely be contacted by many companies that will want to provide various services for you. Many of these companies, in my opinion, only take your money.

Using David Pressman's book as a guide, I did an in-depth patent search and then prepared a US patent application. I followed the instructions, and I obtained the status of patent pending for my new invention.

"Patent pending" status lets all interested parties know that your product is being examined for a US Patent. It does not offer protection as such, but it does strongly suggest that if a patent is awarded in the near future anyone manufacturing the product will more than likely have to stop production.

The patent pending application is not public and therefore other companies cannot see how to produce your product.

If you obtain a US patent, it is only valid in the United States. It offers no protection from infringement in other countries.

If you wish to patent your invention in other countries around the world, you must apply to each and every one of them. This is all but impossible except for large multinational corporations. It is necessary to pay independent maintenance fees for all you patent in overseas countries.

Each country has different laws. In some countries, it is first to file that determines the patent holder.

Every Tuesday the patent office publishes the *Electronic Official Gazette* at: http://www.uspto.gov/web/patents/patog/ that has all the newly awarded US patents. Every country in the world has a representative send the information to their department of commerce or appropriate office.

New patents include detailed drawings and written directions for manufacture of the product. Many times overseas companies just simply start making the new product in their factories for sale in their own country. They are prohibited from selling the patented product in the US, but this does not stop them from making a nice profit in their own country.

American entrepreneurs have been furnishing the rest of the world innovative ideas and products that have made other people billions of dollars for many years and have not received a cent in return.

Chapter 5

Creating the Best Business Structure

At the time you are spending money to obtain a prototype, you will want to legally deduct business expenses. To do this, you will need certain business permits and licenses.

Below, I've given a very helpful web site. All entrepreneurs should study it.
http://www.irs.gov/newsroom/article/0,,id=16949 0,00.html

The Internal Revenue Service reminds taxpayers to follow appropriate guidelines when determining whether an activity is a business or a hobby. Remember, a hobby is an activity not engaged in for profit.

Incorrect deduction of hobby expenses accounts for a portion of the overstated adjustments, deductions, exemptions and credits that add up to $30 billion per year in unpaid taxes, according to IRS estimates.

You may deduct ordinary and necessary expenses for conducting a trade or business. An ordinary expense is an expense that is common and accepted in the taxpayer's trade or business. A necessary expense is one that is appropriate for the business.

Generally, an activity qualifies as a business if it is carried on with the reasonable expectation of earning a profit.

In order to make this determination, taxpayers should consider the following 8 factors quoted from the IRS web page: http://www.irs.gov/

- Does the time and effort put into the activity indicate an intention to make a profit?
- Does the taxpayer depend on income from the activity?
- If there are losses, are they due to circumstances beyond the taxpayer's control or did they occur in the start-up phase of the business?
- Has the taxpayer changed methods of operation to improve profitability?
- Does the taxpayer or his/her advisors have the knowledge needed to carry on the activity as a successful business?

- Has the taxpayer made a profit in similar activities in the past?
- Does the activity make a profit in some years?
- Can the taxpayer expect to make a profit in the future from the appreciation of assets used in the activity?

Forms of Ownership

One of the first decisions that you will have to make as a business owner is how the company should be structured.

This decision will have long-term implications, so consult with an accountant and an attorney to help you select the form of ownership that is right for you.

There are four types of ownership: Sole proprietorship, Partnership, Corporation and Limited Liability Company.

In making a choice, you will want to take into account the following:

- Your vision regarding the size and nature of your business.
- The level of control you wish to have.
- The level of structure you are willing to deal with.

- The business' vulnerability to lawsuits.
- Tax implications of the different ownership structures.
- Expected profit (or loss) of the business.
- Whether or not you need to reinvest earnings into the business.
- Your need for access to cash out of the business for yourself.

Sole Proprietorships

The vast majority of small businesses start out as sole proprietorships. One person, usually the individual who has the day-to-day responsibilities for running the business, owns the firm. Sole proprietors own all the assets of the business and the profits generated by it. They also assume complete responsibility for any of its liabilities or debts. In the eyes of the law and the public, the owner is one in the same with the business.

Advantages of a Sole Proprietorship

- Easiest and least expensive form of ownership to organize.
- Sole proprietors are in complete control, and within the parameters of the law, may make decisions as they see fit.

- Sole proprietors receive all income generated by the business to keep or reinvest.
- Profits from the business flow directly to the owner's personal tax return.
- The business is easy to dissolve, if desired.

Disadvantages of a Sole Proprietorship

- Responsible for all debts against the business.
- Their business and personal assets are at risk.
- May be at a disadvantage in raising funds.
- Often limited to using funds from personal savings or consumer loans.
- May have a hard time attracting high-caliber employees or those who are motivated by the opportunity to own a part of the business.
- Some employee benefits, such as owner's medical insurance premiums, are not directly deductible from business income (only partially deductible as an adjustment to income).

Partnerships

In a partnership, two or more people share ownership of a single business. Like with proprietorships, the law does not distinguish between the business and its owners. The partners should have a legal agreement that sets forth how decisions will be made, profits will be shared, disputes will be resolved, how future partners will be admitted to the partnership, how partners can be bought out, and what steps will be taken to dissolve the partnership when needed.

Yes, it's hard to think about a breakup when the business is just getting started, but many partnerships split up at crisis times, and unless there is a defined process, there will be even greater problems and risk to the overall business.

Partners also must decide up-front how much time and capital each will contribute, etc.

Advantages of a Partnership

- Partnerships are relatively easy to establish, however, time should be invested in developing the partnership agreement.

- With more than one owner, the ability to raise funds may be increased.
- The profits from the business flow directly through to the partners' personal tax returns.
- Prospective employees may be attracted to the business if given the incentive to become a partner.
- The business usually will benefit from partners who have complementary skills.

Disadvantages of a Partnership

- Partners are jointly and individually liable for the actions of the other partners.
- Profits must be shared with others.
- Since decisions are shared, disagreements can occur.
- Some employee benefits are not deductible from business income on tax returns.
- The partnership may have a limited life; it may end upon the withdrawal or death of a partner.

Types of Partnerships that should be considered:

General Partnership

- Partners divide responsibility for management and liability, as well as the shares of profit or loss, according to their internal agreement. Equal shares are assumed unless there is a written agreement that states differently.

Limited Partnership and Partnership with Limited Liability

- Limited means that most of the partners have limited liability (to the extent of their investment) as well as limited input regarding management decisions, which generally encourages investors for short-term projects or for investing in capital assets. This form of ownership is not often used for operating retail or service businesses. Forming a limited partnership is more complex and formal than that of a general partnership.

Joint Venture

- A joint venture acts like a general partnership but is clearly for a limited period of time or a single project. If the partners in a joint venture repeat the activity, they will be recognized as an ongoing partnership and will have to file as such as well as distribute accumulated partnership assets upon dissolution of the entity.

Corporations

A corporation, chartered by the state in which it is headquartered, is considered by law to be a unique entity, separate and apart from those who own it. A corporation can be taxed. It can be sued, and it can enter into contractual agreements. The owners of a corporation are its shareholders. The shareholders elect a board of directors to oversee the major policies and decisions. The corporation has a life of its own and does not dissolve when ownership changes.

Advantages of a Corporation

- Shareholders have limited liability for the corporation's debts or judgments against the corporations.

- Generally, shareholders can only be held accountable for their investment in stock of the company. (Note, however, that officers can be held personally liable for their actions, such as the failure to withhold and pay employment taxes.)
- Corporations can raise additional funds through the sale of stock.
- A corporation may deduct the cost of benefits it provides to officers and employees.
- Can elect S corporation status if certain requirements defined in the section on S corporations are met. This election enables the company to be taxed similar to a partnership.

Disadvantages of a Corporation

- The process of incorporation requires more time and money than other forms of organization.
- Corporations are monitored by federal, state and some local agencies, and as a result more

paperwork may be required to comply with regulations. Many times monthly, quarterly and yearly forms are required.

- Incorporating may result in higher overall taxes. Dividends paid to shareholders are not deductible from business income. Thus it can be taxed twice.

Subchapter S Corporations

This is a tax election only. This election enables the shareholder to treat the earnings and profits as distributions and have them pass through directly to their personal tax return.

The catch here is that the shareholder, if working for the company, and if there is a profit, must pay him/herself wages, and must meet standards of "reasonable compensation.

This can vary by geographical region as well as occupation, but the basic rule is to pay yourself what you would have to pay someone to do your job, as long as there is enough profit. If you do not do this, the IRS can reclassify all of the earnings and profit as wages, and you will be liable for all of the payroll taxes on the total amount.

Limited Liability Company (LLC)

The LLC is a relatively new type of hybrid business structure that is now permissible in most states.

It is designed to provide the limited liability features of a corporation and the tax efficiencies and operational flexibility of a partnership. Formation is more complex and formal than that of a general partnership.
The owners are members, and the duration of the LLC is usually determined when the organization papers are filed.

The time limit can be continued, if desired, by a vote of the members at the time of expiration. LLCs must not have more than two of the four characteristics that define corporations: limited liability to the extent of assets, continuity of life, centralization of management, and free transferability of ownership interests.

You should consult an attorney and an accountant to advise you about the best business structure for you.

Ask for references and talk to more than one accountant and one attorney before selecting an advisor. Ask your family and friends for recommendations. It is a also a good idea to ask small businesses in your area who they use or recommend.

The rule of thumb is as long as a company is losing money, it is advisable to be a sole proprietor. When a company becomes profitable, it is time to a form of corporation.

This is because losses of a sole proprietorship flow through to your personal income tax. Profits in a corporation are generally taxed at a lower rate.

You can start out as one and change to another at a later date. There are other considerations such as personal liability, and this issue is best discussed with a business attorney and accountant.

You will need to obtain the permits and or licenses you will need to start your business. This includes the permits and licenses on the local, county, state, and federal levels.

Go to your city or county occupational license department or county clerk department. Tell them the nature of your new business.

They will advise you about the necessary

licenses and how to apply for them. They can direct you to the state office or web site where you can apply and receive your state license. Most occupational licenses can be obtained online today.

Home offices are accepted in most areas; however, some restrictions may apply. If you live in a zoned residential area, you may need to use a mail P.O. Box and perhaps a storage area for any stock and shipping activities. Most cities and towns have information readily available on their web sites.

It is advisable to fill out and record the Doing Business As (DBA and or fictitious name application so you can operate under names associated under your trademark.

An Employer Identification Number (EIN) is also known as a Federal Tax Identification Number and is used to identify a business entity. Generally, businesses need an EIN. You may apply for an EIN in various ways, such as online at: http://www.irs.gov/. There is no cost for this number which is issued by the Internal Revenue Service. Check with your state Department of Revenue to apply for your state identification number or charter that may be needed to collect and pay state sales tax.

You may need an EIN number for things like opening up a business checking account.

You should use some type of accounting software from the beginning to keep track of your income and expenses. Quick Books ® or Peachtree Accounting® are very good and are relatively inexpensive. Software will enable you to create invoices, purchase orders, credit memos, and other forms from built-in templates. These forms will look professional and will be filed so you can refer to them in the future.

It is also valuable to use an e-mail system to keep track and record all e-mail related to your business.

Chapter 6

Do I Need a Business Plan?

It is advisable to create a business plan. The first business plan you create does not have to be extensive. It can even be in outline form for your eyes only.

In the early stages of my company, my business plan was an outline along with a checklist. This checklist had a timetable of things I needed to accomplish to start my business.

Certainly, if your goal is to raise a large sum of money for a new start-up company, you will need to develop a strong business plan.

I am more in favor of a self-financed business start up as described in my chapter about financing a new business.

You will add to and change your business plan as your company develops. I often create a new business or marketing plan whenever I start an extensive campaign. This helps me stay focused.

There are several places to receive free or low cost help with writing your business plan. They are:

SBA: Small Business Administration: www.sba.gov/starting_business /planning/writingplan.html

SBDC: Small Business Development Center Go to www.sba.gov/sbds to find your local office.

SCORE: www.score.org

Also check with your local university or college. Many graduate students in business schools will develop your plan for course credit.

Go to your local inventor club. Many members will share ideas and introduce you to free help.

The Internet is full of free forms, including business plan templates.

Later in your company's development, you will modify or create new business plans as your needs and goals change. In the beginning, just write a document that answers the questions who, where, when, why and how.

Chapter 7

Will My Product Sell?

In the beginning, you will not know if your product will sell in the marketplace. There is no way to predict if a product will sell well.

Many people have tried and many people have failed to predict product sales. The US Patent and Trademark Office is filled with thousands of amazing product patents that never sold despite gallant and well-financed efforts.

You must TEST, TEST and TEST your product to determine marketability. You do not want to spend a lot of money and time on a product if it will not sell. I recommend a three-to-six month trial period. If you put all your effort into a product for six months and have not at least covered your costs, then perhaps, you should move on to the next idea.

On the other hand, if you have covered your cost up to that point, and the product shows great potential based on results and reactions by customers, then you should proceed at full speed and from that point on do not take "no" for an answer. Give it one hundred percent of your effort.

The first step in bringing a new product to market is to sell or even give away some of your products. Ask for feedback. Generally, people will give their opinions freely about products. Your family is a good source for advice, but remember at this stage those closest to you may tell you what you want to hear. You need feedback from customers and potential customers. If you start to hear things like, "I wish I thought of that," "You're going to sell a million of these," and "You're going to be a millionaire," you may have a successful product on your hands.

My plan was to wear, give away, and sell as many of my initial order of 200 pins as I could. Then I sat back and waited to see if people would contact me for more. I thought of this as a trial period to determine if I wanted to invest the time and money to start a business based on my new invention.

During this time, I began to read as many books as I could about marketing, patents, trademarks, and small business.

All of our 200 pins were sold or given away in a short time and my cost was more than covered.

Within 3 weeks, several dozen people who wanted more CLIPEZE Badge Holders contacted me. I then had 500 CLIPEZE pins manufactured. Again, about 2 weeks later, several dozen more people called me wanting more. I cut the trial period short and manufactured 1,000 badge holder pins.

By then, I had completed reading many business books and applied for and received my local, state and federal business permits and licenses required for a home business.

At this point, I had enough earnings to buy a new computer and put up a web site. Remember, this was 1995 and not many companies were on the web. I found a friend who had made a web site for his church, and he was happy to set up a site for CLIPEZE for free.

Today, many sites, such as http://www.godaddy.com/, have templates to make your own web site construction much easier and for very little cost.

For the first year, our web site was just a basic billboard type of site that only had our name, address and phone numbers and a picture or two of the product, but I was on the web! Just being on the web in 1995 was like being a pioneer of a new technology!

Trade shows are wonderful for assessing your product's ability to sell. Trade shows are expensive, but exhibiting at a show will allow you to directly explain your product and see and hear the reaction to your product. You get instant feedback. More on trade shows later in the book, as they are a great means to market your product.

Setting prices

Setting the price of your new product can have a direct bearing on product sales. Basically, setting prices is an art, not a science.

Many factors come into play when you set prices.

- Cost plus margin: You must take into consideration the cost to manufacture and the price needed to make an acceptable profit margin.
- Competition: What are other companies charging for similar products? If there are no products in

the market like yours, you are free to set the standard.

- Comparisons: How is your product different from other products on the market? Does it offer advantages, such as saving time or greater efficiency than anything on the market?
- Premium quality or value: If you offer a premium product, you will command a high price. An example of this is Bayer® Aspirin. Bayer represents quality. Several store brands have the very same ingredients and are located on the shelf next to Bayer® Aspirin, but people pay more for the perceived higher quality.
- How difficult to duplicate. Take into consideration how hard it is for another company to duplicate your product.
- Benefits to customers: If your product or service offers great new benefits to customers, you can command higher prices.
- Cost of acquiring new customers: Determine how difficult marketing to your niche will be and factor this into your price structure.

Consumer Psychology Pricing

No place illustrates the differences in psychology pricing better than the cosmetic or perfume industry. Prices. The mark up on these products can be over 200%.

Does perfume that retails for $100.00 an ounce cost more to produce than one that sells for $10.00 an ounce? They both smell very good. Maybe the expensive perfume does cost more to produce, but more than likely, it does not.

The price difference may be because the customer views the more expensive one as superior or perhaps they will be admired by friends when they use or buy the more expensive perfume.

Prices may work differently if you change the category your product is in. In the case of our company, we tested our product for pricing in several ways.

When displayed in a retail store individually packaged on a card, our product retails for about $5.00. At this price, it appeals to department heads or managers who want to give a good low-cost gift to all their employees. It appeals to the human resources department buyers who want a low-priced, quality item for all 1,000 employees at their facility. It also appeals to the individual as an impulse item at the counter of the store.

When we tested our product packaged in an upscale jewelry box with the price of $19.95, we targeted the product as a single gift for a special friend.

And when we packaged it together with matching earrings retailing for $39.99, the focus was on being a very special gift a man would buy for his wife to mark a special occasion.

The best thing to do is test all categories to come up with the best price for your new product. You also need to test the best way to sell your product. Most products evolve naturally, but testing is the only way to find what works for your product.

Your three choices are retail, wholesale, or both retail and wholesale. Certainly the type and sales price of your product can dictate how you will sell.

Retail Sales

Retail is selling directly to the consumer or end user. The advantage of selling this way is that you get full retail price and gain a high margin on sales of your product.

You sell retail by store, online web site, flea market, Kiosk, word of mouth, direct mail, ads in magazines and newspapers, or a combination of these.

If you have a heavy industrial product, say for example a new energy efficient home heating or cooling system that sells for $10,000 with a 50% margin, you may be successful selling retail locally at a store and placing ads in your local newspaper.

If you have a low-priced product that only nets you a few dollars, you will use a different tactic, such as selling online from your web site.

There are several disadvantages to selling only retail. Stores and kiosks have high overhead expenses and the hours are very long. Startup costs are very high and you are dependant on local economic conditions.

Direct mail and space ads usually offer the best way to sell direct to end-users.

Wholesale Sales

Selling wholesale is when you sell to re-sellers, such as catalogs and retail stores. They, in turn, resell your products to the end user.

The disadvantage of selling wholesale is you sell your product at a lower price, However, you generally sell many more units wholesale.

The hours needed to sell by wholesale are much better as orders can be filled anytime of the day or night. It is even possible to contract out to a fulfillment warehouse that can pack and ship your orders for you.

Both Retail and Wholesale

Most entrepreneurs sell both retail and wholesale. As a matter of fact, selling just wholesale for single product producers is fast becoming a thing of the past.

The biggest problem you will have is that some of your re-sellers may view you as competition for customers. Re-sellers generally want to sell your product at a 100 percent profit. This is referred in the retail business as keystone pricing. For example, they buy your product for 50 dollars and sell it for 100 dollars. It is advisable to keep your retail prices about 10 percent higher than the keystone price or the MSRP (Manufacturers Suggested Retail Price). You still will get many customers who do not have access to your re-sellers and still protect your re-sellers suggested retail price.

If a re-seller asks you about selling directly to

the public, you simply answer the question with a question: Why would your customer come to us to buy when they can buy it from your store at a cheaper price?

We were successful in my business in obtaining wholesale sales in direct mail catalogs early on. Our products were purchased by customers who then went to our web site to view and purchase new or other designs that could not be found in the catalog.

Marketing Begets Marketing

Everything you do comes together to make sales.
Some customers will purchase your product the first time they see it. Others may see it in a catalog or store and call you to get a brochure then go to your web site and make a purchase.

Chapter 8
Financing a New Business

Start slowly and develop the business one step at a time rather than borrowing money to start a home business. If possible, market your business from what you earn from it. Sell 100 units of your product and then buy 200 more. Sell the 200 and buy 400. Go slowly.

Begin small. Keep your "day job" and live on the earnings of your current employment. Use the proceeds from your business to build growth. It is a good idea not to leave your day job until you have a year's gross pay from your salaried job in the bank.

Some entrepreneurs believe that you need twenty, thirty or even fifty thousand dollars to start a business. I don't agree and my company's success proves it. I will say that the start-up cost greatly depends on the type of product you have. For example, if your product requires a plastic mold, you will need funds to create one.

Pay these vendors as you go. Do not let debt mount in the early stages of your business.

Later in your company's development, I have found that the best financing deals come to you. After you reach *patent pending* status or sell your first item, create and send out a press release. See the chapter on marketing and the resources in the back of this book to learn how to create outstanding press releases that get published for free.

Local banks and lending sources always read the local papers. You will probably be contacted after your press release because a story about a local person creating a new product always creates interest. When banks or lending sources ask you for an appointment, remember: be very careful with debt.

Borrowing should be done with extreme caution. Debt can be very hard to overcome and can sink your home business before it can get off the ground.

Use your time and effort, instead of money, when starting a home business. Do as much as you can yourself. By doing this, you will know every part of the process of your business and will make the most of the resources you have.

Be careful buying office furniture and supplies. Check local flea markets, garage sales or yard sales for your needs. They only need to be functional. Don't get carried away with appearance, and remind yourself that every dollar saved should go into the business to finance growth.

Consider bartering or trading some of your products or services for items or services you require. This can be very effective if a company you need services from can use your product as an incentive or premium.

There are some essentials you must have to run a business in today's market place. If you do not have a working knowledge of computers or an understanding of the resources of the Internet, you will need to learn them as soon as possible. You will need this knowledge even before you have a prototype of your product made. Check your nearest community college or ask your small business development center for information where you can attend classes.

Play up your strengths and play down your weaknesses. Many people like doing business with small businesses. Focus on the strength that you can give special attention to your customer's needs. You can make fast decisions without checking with a boss, colleagues, or directors.

I cannot stress the debt issue enough. There are several books out by very wealthy individuals who state that there is good debt and bad debt.

They claim good debt is debt they need to start a business or buy rental property and is repaid by customers or renters. I agree that debt has a place in a business after it reaches a certain level but not for a home-based start-up company. Later, for example, you may want to have a credit line to help with trends that require capital one time of year, but when you collect your receivables later in the year, you must pay the credit line balance off.

If you land a large sale before you are ready, don't worry. You can always do factoring. Factoring is the process whereby a company sells its accounts receivable to a factoring company at a discount and receives cash. If you have a substantial order from a large company, it is an easy process.

Companies that do factoring advertise in small business magazines. Your local bank can refer you to a company to help with your factoring needs. Another strategy is to offer your customer a discount for prepayment or charge a deposit to pay your cost.

Even though I strongly am in favor of self-financing your business, every product and service is different and you should be aware of some other ways to finance a business.

The best way to find the groups or institutions in the following sections is to contact your local small business association. To find your nearest local offices go to: http://www.sba.gov/localresources/index.html.

Angel Investors

Angel investors are investors, or a small group of investors, that look for high-growth companies in a particular industry. They look for an industry that they have experienced huge success with in the past, or are now experiencing great success with.

These investors look for companies that offer products or services that the other companies they have an interest in can benefit from.

For example, if you invented a product that every hospital in the US would readily purchase and benefit from, and an angel investor controls 5,000 hospitals, the angel investor would be extremely interested in your company. The angel may own a stake in a large medical product distributing company. So, by investing in your company the angel's hospitals, distribution company and his stake in your company all will, more than likely, grow as they all do business together.

Angel investors do not give you "free money" and their involvement can be expensive. The angel investor will more than likely require 10 to 50 percent equity or ownership of your company.

Many times, they also charge a management fee or retainer. Sometimes they require the placement of a board member on your board of directors if you have a corporation. They may require a new general manager for your business. This secures their investment but you lose some control of your business.

Angels usually invest between $300,000 and $5 million per company. A list of Angels or Angel Investor Groups can be obtained from your local small business association.

Finance a Company from Your Retirement or 401-k Account.

A 401(k) is a tax-deferred savings and retirement fund set up by employers. This account can be used for start-up capital. In many cases, there are substantial penalties for early withdrawal. Some plans allow for loans based on your 401(k) balance. In effect, you are borrowing your own money from your fund. Your plan administrator can advise you as to the term length and interest rate you will pay.

Borrow on the Equity of Your Home.

It is easy to borrow on the equity of your home, as you can control the amount needed and the repayment terms. Shop around for the best deal. This is widely done to get capital to start a business.

You will have monthly payments and this will put pressure on your new business to obtain a certain sales volume to pay the payments.

Depending on current mortgage rates you may be able to refinance at a lower rate than your first mortgage and take some funds out and keep your payments low.

Borrow Against Insurance Policies

Each month, you may pay for several kinds of insurance policies. You can only borrow against whole life insurance, but many policies have some cash value after a few years.

All you need to do is contact your insurance agent. Tell him you are interested in taking out a policy loan. Many companies will lend up to 90% of the cash value of the policy.

As long as you continue to pay the premiums, your insurance coverage continues. Keep in mind that if you die with a policy loan outstanding, the benefits might be reduced. One advantage of this kind of financing is a low interest rate. This is because most of the interest rate is tied to the money-market rate.

Credit Cards

Credit cards are easy credit. Using a credit card is a great way to buy some inventory or to get a prototype made. Certainly care should be used to make sure balances don't climb.

I started my company CLIPEZE by buying 200 units with a credit card. I sold them and paid my balance and bought 400 units, etc.

If you can find a credit card with a good rewards program, it can help later when you need to do some traveling to market your products or services.

Family and Friends

Sometimes you know someone or have a family member who has an interest in seeing you succeed and has the ability to lend you funds. Many times it is a person who has had or has a business and wants to help you be successful as well. They believe in you and/or your product.

I recommend that if you borrow from friends or family, you create a written contract. You want to make sure that both parties understand the terms of the loan. You don't want a loan that is going to be repaid and terminated to be misunderstood as a partnership or as equity in your company.

Bank Term and SBA Loans

It is my experience that a bank term and an SBA loan are, in fact, one and the same. Most banks only give term loans to companies already in business that have shown financial strength. Your company's financial strength requirement varies from bank to bank for these loans. These term loans usually carry a fixed rate of interest.

The federal government, which has abundant funds and programs, backs the SBA loans but most of the same banks that issue their own term loans are also SBA lenders.

Your company does not apply directly to the SBA for SBA loans. You apply to the bank and the bank obtains the SBA loan. The banks use the same standards for SBA as their own term loans. The only thing they do is approve some SBA loans backed by the government to earn processing fees and stay in government programs so they can advertise as full-service business lenders.

The government funds that have been earmarked for new or start-up companies rarely get to them. The funds only reach companies that can otherwise qualify for regular term business loans.

According to the N.F.I.B (National Federation of Independent Businesses) less than 1 % of small businesses receive SBA loans.

Private Guarantee Loans

A private guarantee load is when an angel investor or wealthy individual guarantees a loan from a bank or other institution. These guarantee loans are unusual, but sometimes they are used for a year or two until the new company has enough revenue to raise capital to repay the loan.

Royalty-based Loans

A royalty-based loan is an advance of funds to be paid back by a percentage of future sales or revenue. Most of the time this is done with established companies or companies that are about to launch a new high-margin product into the market place. Usually royalty financing appeals to investors who do not make a lot of investments into private companies.

Several colleges and universities have made royalty deals with new products that they help invent or produce.

I would encourage you to keep this type of financing in mind if you utilize a college or university in the development of your prototype as suggested earlier in this book. One advantage to this type of financing is that most of the time it is considered a loan and does not come under state and federal securities laws.

Chapter 9

Marketing Your Product or Service

I followed Jeffery Dobkin's book *How To Market A Product for Under $500* on marketing (found in the reference section of this book).

I particularly followed the chapter called, "Catalog Campaign". I wrote highly targeted catalog buyers personal letters almost every day. When I wasn't writing them, I was following up with them. Day after day, month after month, I contacted buyers. All the while, I continued selling my products to local people as word of my product spread.

I kept this up for about 6 months without success. I had enough rejection letters to wallpaper my home office wall.

One day, I called one of the catalogs as a follow-up to samples I had sent and the buyer actually answered the phone. I was expecting another rejection when she apologized and said that someone was supposed to call me and that they were going to use my product in their next catalog. I did not change the tone of my voice. When I got off the phone I shouted so loud my wife came running to see if I had had an accident.

After the catalog was dropped (mailed) to several hundred thousand nurses and other medical employees, the orders started to come in. At first, I received a few hundred, then several hundred more, and finally thousands poured in. In all, over 45,000 CLIPEZE badge holder pins were sold in six months by that catalog. It did not stop there.

Other catalogs that hadn't been sure about CLIPEZE in the past called us. A second catalog then sold over 150,000 pins in a six-month period. I took advantage of my good fortune and hard work and created a press release and sent it to local newspapers in the community.

The story was picked up and local sales improved substantially. Our story was widely read and I received other benefits from it.

Several local banks called me and set up appointments to visit with me. I received some calls from freight carriers that led to reduced shipping rates.

Getting in those two catalogs had other benefits. Retail stores noticed our product in the catalogs and some of their customers were asking for them by name so they started to call us. We were asked if we would consider selling wholesale. So we made up a makeshift display and started to sell to some uniform retail stores.

The display was very unsophisticated and consisted of a cardboard backing of a common 8 x 11 easel type picture frame covered with a colorful paper we printed ourselves. We glued the paper to the matting of the frame with spray glue.. We bought as many frames from dollar stores as we could. And yes you are correct, the price was $1.00 each.

Soon, a traveling independent sales representative saw our display in a store. He called to ask if we would consider using independent sales representatives. We said we would and signed him to represent our products throughout the Northeast.

He reported back two weeks later that he had sold our product to every retail store he visited. Soon, we had signed up 8 sales reps, one for every section of the country.

There are several benefits using sales reps.
- No need to pay employees
- Only pay them only when they sell
- They have established relationships with retailers
- Commissions are predictable
- Enter a market immediately
- They provide customer feedback

Make sure you have a written agreement with sales reps, and both parties understand their territorial areas. In our case, our sales reps' exclusive area is for medical uniform stores located in the states traveled by the rep. We do not extend the exclusive rights to other industries in the same areas.

It is a good idea to stipulate that either party can terminate the agreement with a 30-day written notice. Make sure that the sales rep knows he is responsible for returning any samples to you upon termination. List any "house accounts" that are in the areas but serviced by the company directly so that you aren't required to pay a commission on those accounts.

You may be required to send a 1099 tax form to

all reps that earn over $600 in one year. You also are required to transmit the 1099 form to the IRS. This form can be generated with your accounting software. You can ask your accountant to prepare them with your yearly taxes.

Once I started using sales reps, I started putting my product into 100 new stores a month. Including reorders, I soon was shipping over 400 orders a month to both catalogs and retail stores. My products sold very fast. They often sold before the store employees could unpack the boxes and set up the displays.

With boxes for priority mailing stacked from our kitchen table to the ceiling, my wife and I decided that we needed to hire someone to help with packing.

Creating your Press Release

For the first several months you should concentrate on submitting press releases and marketing to direct mail and web catalogs. Press releases have great value. You need to learn how to construct an effective press release and submit it to local, national, and web-based newspapers often. You also need to send press releases to trade publication magazines.

A list of newspapers and magazines with editor's names can be found in several directories, such as *Bacon's Newspaper and Magazine Guide,* located in many public libraries.

As for your local newspaper, simply drop off your press release at the newspaper office. Most have an "in" box set aside for press releases.

If you want to be more aggressive, it is all right to contact a reporter or the editor of your local paper and ask if you can send a release to them personally.

You are advised to study how to write effective press releases. It will help you to read the books listed in the reference section of this book. Make sure your press release is written in the proper form and checked and rechecked for grammar. Often, if the press release is done well, small newspapers will insert the release into their publication exactly as they receive it from you.

You can find help writing press releases in your community. Most newspapers will have someone interested in helping you create press releases for reasonable rates. The communication and journalism departments of a local college are great places to find inexpensive help with your press releases. Most undergraduates or graduate students not only jump at the chance to make extra money, but they have great talent and will give you insight about your products.

The News Observer Newspaper in Titusville, Florida published the newspaper article below from our submitted press release.

FOR IMMEDIATE RELEASE

Release Feb. 2007, # C2-13
For More Information: Gary R. Bronga
President, CLIPEZE
Phone 321-264-7599, Fax 800-314-1075
NO KILL DATE

ENTREPRENEUR DEVELOPS SECOND NEW PRODUCT

About ten years ago businessman Gary

Bronga invented a new product called

CLIPEZE. It is worn like a lapel pin but allows

the attachment of an identification badge.

Today, his product is found in over 1,000 retail

stores and 20 catalogs across the US and Canada, Spain and Switzerland.

He has now developed another original product that has the potential to become even more successful. It is a white medical and professional shoe that has a totally different look. Mr. Bronga has taken his best selling art designs from the CLIPEZE pin line, and then he silk-screened the images directly on the upper part of the shoes. The art images are placed on the shoe in patterns in different directions. The result of initial testing has been outstanding. "We have the potential to start a whole new trend in the professional shoe industry," Gary said.

CLIPEZE, Inc. has contracted the manufacturing to a shoe factory in Asia for the production of the CLOGEZE shoe line. The shoes will be made of the highest quality construction. They will retail for about $35.00.

For more information contact: Gary R. Bronga

P.O. Box 373, Mims, FL 32754.

Phone: 800-385-0014

###

Local papers love stories about one of their residents inventing a new product.

Send releases often. They can be about any subject. Write one about a trade show you are going to or have attended. Or write one about a new retail store that has agreed to carry your product. Enclose a photo of your product. Let everyone know you have filed a patent or have patent pending.

Press releases can do much more than bring in

direct sales. They can bring in the attention of your local bank, freight carriers, printers, and other businesses in your community.

You will, more than likely, be contacted by charities that want donations. It is a good idea to donate to charities even if all you can do is donate your time or offer your best wholesale prices to help with fundraisers. You will not only experience personal fulfillment from being able to support the charities of your choice, you will open the door to meet business leaders in your area.

Press releases sent to trade publications can provide national and even international exposure. You never know who may read about you or where it may lead.

When I started submitting press releases, I was surprised how accepting the reporters and editors were. They are faced with deadlines and a well-written press release makes their jobs easier.

Trade Shows

Trade shows are one of the most valuable marketing tools you can use. As noted earlier, they are also a great way to test market your product before you go into mass production.

Many people you will meet at trade shows are CEOs/presidents or vice presidents of large corporations. Also, you will meet buyers from every business level. Many of these people would never even take your phone call or return a call from you in the normal course of business. Now, they are standing directly in front of you and you have the opportunity to show them your brand new product.

The reason people attend trade shows is to see new products. These shows cost them time and money to attend, and they are in a buying or a business frame of mind. Take advantage of the situation by talking to as many people as you can.

You can identify the trade show where you will want to exhibit in several ways. First, look in trade publications. Many advertise or have articles or ads in the trade publications for upcoming shows. Several trade publications even sponsor shows.

Do a web search for trade shows in your industry. The web site http://www.tsnn.com is very good for finding shows in many industries.

You may also call some buyers who you are targeting and ask which shows they attend and would recommend. Most buyers will be happy to discuss this with you and may help you with any questions about hotels or other questions you have about a show.

Once you identify the shows you would like to exhibit in, contact them and ask for an exhibitor information kit. Read this kit very carefully because you may need to rent a table/chairs/carpet, etc. That can add to the cost of exhibiting. The exhibit manual will have all the facts, prices and pictures of the previous year's show. Booth space is expensive, often costing between $1,200 and $2,500 for a typical 10 x 10 foot space.

There are several ways to keep trade show costs reasonable. One way to cut the price is to go to trade shows near to where you live. This way, you can eliminate the cost of airfare, hotels, and the shipping of your materials. Orlando, Chicago, New York and Las Vegas are the most common cities for trade shows. However, hundreds of shows, both large and small, are held in every major city in the country.

Many shows post their schedules years in advance. You can save a lot of money by waiting months or a year until a certain show comes near your home.

View last year's exhibitor list and see if you do business with any companies attending or if any companies are located near you. If there are, perhaps you can visit them and ask if you can share space at their table and split the cost of the next trade show.

Call and talk to the person in charge of the trade show listed in the exhibitor information kit. Ask this person if they have a first–time exhibitor price or if they know of a company that may want to share the cost of a booth. They may make suggestions to help with cutting costs, such as offering a discount for booking in advance.

Trade show displays are expensive. It is more important to be creative rather than spend a lot of money. A good product and enthusiasm will win out over a huge display every time.

In our early days at CLIPEZE, we used life-size cardboard cutouts of movie stars on which to display our products. These cutouts are the kind found in movie rental stores like Blockbusters®. We bought them online for about $45, and we could pack them in our airline luggage, eliminating shipping fees. We created an identification badge for the cardboard movie star and attached our CLIPEZE badge holder to it. You would be surprised how many people wanted to get their picture taken with "John Wayne" or "Pamela Anderson." The cardboard cutout was very effective for us. Brainstorm with family and friends and use your imagination to see what you can come up with.

Pay attention to details when you travel to trade shows. Booking a flight in the morning is always a good idea. If you have a delay due to weather or some other unavoidable reason you will have a chance to get a later flight. If you book the last flight of the day, and have a delay, you may not arrive on the day you require.

I have seen several exhibitors try to save money by staying at a cheaper hotel only to pay twenty dollars or more each way by cab for transportation to the convention centers while the participation hotels generally have free shuttles. Do your homework to save money.

Since tradeshows are an expensive investment, get the most value from them by attending personally. You, as the company owner, need to be at all the trade shows and present all the time. Employees or family/friends certainly can be a great help, but you know your product better than anyone. You need to be available to land that big deal when it presents itself. You would be surprised how many times I have seen employees turn their backs on potential customers to play games or check e-mail on a laptop computer. Meanwhile, major company buyers walk by the booth.

Develop your sales speech so you are ready for business. Recite it over and over again. Soon you will have what is called an Elevator Speech, which is a speech you can make to describe your product and its benefits in the time it takes to ride an elevator with a complete stranger.

Create a sample kit. This should include brochures, product information, prices and actual samples if possible. Be sure you always have approximately twelve sample kits when you attend every trade show. Additionally, always have several hundred business cards available to be handed to potential buyers.

You should always make sure you have a few press releases with you because reporters from trade publication usually cover the trade show. You will see them walking around taking photos of attendees and exhibitors.

One way to attract sales representatives at a show is to place a small sign on your table that reads "Sales Reps Wanted." Sales representatives will notice the sign right away but just as important, an attendee may refer you to a sales rep that is not at the show.

Talk to everyone. This includes other exhibitors. They can provide a wealth of information including information about other shows.

When you register for a trade show, ask if there is a drawing or there are door prizes for the attendees. Participate, and give one of your products for the raffle, unless it is cost prohibitive of course.

Most trade shows have a new product showcase and many times it is free to new exhibitors. This attracts many attendees.

Many distribution agreements are formed between exhibitors at shows. If your product can be sold to exhibitor companies, give them the sales pitch but do it at a time when they do not have prospects in their booth. Exhibitors also can identify very important buyers or sales representatives who may be interested in representing your products.

Always remember that you never really know who you are talking to and where a conversation can lead when conversing with people at a trade show.

I always talk to the trade show hall staff, including the cleaning staff. Once I gave a sample of our product to an electrician who was hooking up electricity to my booth. Later, the man returned with his union representative and they ordered a custom CLIPEZE badge holder for every member of the local union. I covered the cost of that entire show with just this one sale.

We have exhibited our CLIPEZE products in over 100-trade shows. We once exhibited in 27 shows in a 24-month period.

The shows we exhibited in were both big and small. Some lasted a week in the largest exhibit halls in the country and others just lasted a few hours in the local hotel ballroom across town. We set goals for every show. At some shows, we sell our products on the spot. While in other shows, we concentrate on capturing leads. The feedback we have received at most shows is incredible.

The reactions we received left little doubt that we had a great product. It is a wonderful feeling to be in a booth with people four or five deep with dollar bills in their hands eagerly waiting to make a purchase of your invention.

I have learned that little things make a big difference. Look people in the eye when you speak to them. Have an honest belief in your product.

Execute a firm handshake. These things can result in success.

Actions, like standing at your booth, make you much more approachable than sitting in a chair. Keep a friendly smile on your face. How you dress can make a difference. In Orlando or Las Vegas, which are vacation capitals, the dress is casual. Shows in Chicago and New York require more formal business attire.

One suggestion is to buy a uniform of sorts, such as Docker® type pants and a matching shirt with the company logo or product name on it. This is much cheaper and more comfortable than formal wear and gives you an opportunity to show your logo even when you are out of your booth.

Most of the time, it is advisable to use the preferred freight carrier for shipping your display and supplies to the trade show you are attending. Trade show halls and union rules and regulations make it difficult for other freight carriers to ship in and out of the trade show facilities. You usually can set up an account with the preferred carrier by following directions in the exhibitor's handbook.

Find out about recommended ground transportation. You can find ground transportation information in your exhibitor handbook or by calling the hotel where you will be staying. Some hotels offer free shuttle buses to and from the airport.

Once in Chicago at a large show with over 500 exhibitors and thousands of attendees, my display booth and all my samples and merchandise got lost during shipping. For that show, I had decided to use a new freight carrier. They were several hundred dollars cheaper than the show's preferred carrier. You guessed it. When the show opened, there I was standing behind my table without anything other than a few catalogs and the samples I had carried on the plane in my briefcase.

I stood without my product or display and gave my sales speech for three days, I actually made some sales and collected several valuable leads that converted into sales at a later date. My display and inventory arrived on the third and final day just in time for me to ship it back to our office.

Always think success and you will find it. Talk enthusiastically about your product. Listen to what attendees say. Gauge their reactions to your product. You will hear the same questions time and time again. This enables you to create flyers and direct mail pieces that answer their questions.

Another reason to listen is that people often give you new ideas on how to improve your product or even for the creation of new products. This interaction between attendees and exhibitors is very valuable. When the doors open and the people all walk onto the trade show floor, you will receive feedback almost immediately.

A very good show to exhibit in is the Invention & New Product Exposition National Tradeshow held annually in Pittsburgh. If you cannot exhibit in this show, you should attend for networking purposes. They have several seminars and guest speakers at this show who may help you make your product successful. See more information at www.inpex.com.

I would advise you to read as many books about trade show strategy as you can. Trade show marketing is one of the best ways to grow your business. It is a great way to multiply your network.

Don't hesitate to start conversations with attendees as they pass by. Some will avoid you and keep walking. Some will stop and be so surprised at your product that they will buy it on the spot or thank you for stopping them and explaining your product to them.

Additionally, try to always have a "Special Show Price" sale. This gives attendees an incentive to buy at the show.

Be on the lookout for trade show attendees who do not want anything other than free samples of products. Many times they are not even in business themselves. You'll see many of these folks, and you'll usually see them pulling a rolling carrier filled with the free samples they have collected.

One note of warning. Safeguard valuable products at trade shows. With thousands of people in attendance, there is a good possibility you'll be distracted. This can lead to theft. Most trade show halls are secured during off hours, but most shows do not guarantee security. See the show exhibitor handbook for details.

Chapter 10

Direct Marketing

Wikipedia, which is a wonderful free, web encyclopedia and found at: http://en.wikipedia.org/, defines direct marketing as a sub-discipline and type of marketing.

The term *direct marketing* is believed to have been first used in 1967 by Lester Wunderman. Mr. Wunderman is known as the father of direct marketing.

There are two main definitional characteristics of direct marketing that distinguish it from other types of marketing. The first is that it attempts to send its messages directly to consumers, without the use of intervening media. This involves unsolicited commercial communication (direct mail, e-mail, telemarketing) with consumers or businesses.

The second characteristic is that it is focused on deriving a specific call-to-action This aspect of direct marketing involves an emphasis on measurable positive (but not negative) responses from consumers (known simply as *response* in the industry) regardless of medium. If the advertisement asks the prospect to take a specific action (for instance, call a toll free number or visit a website), then the effort is considered to be direct-response advertising.

Another form of marketing is informative marketing. Usually, only large multinational corporations do this type of marketing. An example of informative marketing would be the Coca-Cola® TV commercials. The purpose is not to sell directly, but to reinforce the brand name.

In bringing a product to market, you need to learn all you can to become a master direct marketer.

Direct Mail

After my company was successful at getting our products into catalogs and retail stores, direct mail was the next logical step. Our market was not well defined by our early success.

Armed with Jeff Dobkin's book *How to Market a Product for Under $500* we created our first direct mail piece.
We contacted the list broker Dunhill List Co. Cindy Dunhill is extremely well known, respected, knowledgeable, and also very helpful. The Dunhill web site is www.dunhills.com. By renting the complete list of the entire medical uniform store in the US and Canada, we were able to reach many stores that our sales representatives did not.

Ms. Dunhill compared the list with our growing in-house list and eliminated duplicate names, so we only bought new store names. A good list broker will go over the rate card, which is a record of the list, and can see what companies rented the list in the past. If a past renter is a company that targets the same customers as you do, it may be a good list to test. Additionally if a list is rented several times by companies, it shows that the list may have some merit.

The best thing about direct mail is that it is predictable and measurable. Basically, if you have a qualified list of, say, 20,000 names and you mail to 2,000 of them, you can measure the results and predict the results of future mailings.

If, as in this example, you have a net return on investment of $200 when you send to 2,000; then you can predict that if you send the same mail piece to 4,000 names, you will make double that amount. There have been many successful businesses built using just this strategy alone.

Testing Direct Mail

Testing is the key to direct mail. It is strongly advised that you read Appendix 2 which contains a copy of a white paper by Robert Dunhill, President of Dunhill International List Co.

Space Ads and Classified Ads

The best way I have found to use space or classified ads is in conjunction with a press release. When a magazine or newspaper prints an editorial article about your company from one of your submitted press releases, you can gauge the response.

If you have a large response from a story it may be a good idea to follow up and run a space ad or classified ad in the months following the story.

Some trade publications will even sell you a package offering to do an editorial story on your product and sell you an ad in the same or subsequent issues, while others will deny any connection between the editorial and advertising departments. However, don't let anyone tell you differently. The editorial and advertising departments are connected.

It is advisable to contact all the trade publications in your industry and ask for a Media Kit, the current issue, and one past issue of the publication. You can find phone numbers for their department of advertising in *Bacon's Newspaper and Magazine Guide* or other such informational guides. A media kit gives you the breakdown and cost for placing an ad as well as circulation, demographics and other facts and figures.

You will find that ads are proportionally as expensive the more times a year that you place them in a publication. You will pay more for one ad (or for 1X) than for an ad placed in every month of a year (12 X.)

As pointed out later in the chapter about negotiation, the 12 X price will cover the magazine or newspaper's cost plus a little margin and is always where I start my negotiation.

A side benefit of requesting a media kit is that you generally will become a qualified member in your industry and receive a free subscription to the magazine. This saves you a lot of money and helps you stay informed as to where to send press releases.

Magazines try to base their advertising rates on both paid and free subscription circulation figures so they want to give you a subscription as much as you want one.

A 15-Point Checklist for Your Ad

The article titled *A 15-Point Checklist for Your Ad* and the article about *Increasing Response Rates of Ads and Direct Mail through Imaginative Booklet Titles* by Jeffrey Dobkin are reproduced in Appendix 3. Jeffrey is a master direct marketer. You can obtain more information and see other valuable articles at: http://www.dobkin.com/

Marketing with Tips Booklets

Another successful manner to market is to utilize tips booklets. For instance my *48-Great Tips for Bringing a New Product to Market from Your Home* was helpful in promoting this book. The size of this booklet is 8.5" x 3.5".. The booklet's weight in an envelope is just less than one ounce to allow for first class letter postage.

My booklet was produced by Paulette Ensign who is the founder and chief visionary of www.tipsbooklets.com.
The article below, found on Paulette Ensign's web site, is a wonderful strategy for driving qualified traffic to a web site:

I am not a web designer or search engine optimizer, nor do I play one on TV. However, I do know that the driving force in bringing qualified traffic to your web site is dynamic high value content. That means compelling, interesting, approachable, and immediately useful information, especially when you also directly sell products or services at your site. Increasing and maintaining traffic also demands both offline and online mechanisms to attract those visitors.

One of the easiest and most versatile forms of the content described above is a 'how-to' tips booklet. With the right writing style, not only can you use the booklet in its entirety as a downloadable bonus file on your site, it can also be sliced, diced, and reformatted to get the most mileage possible from the single document.

Imagine a booklet called "110 Ways to Get the Most Out of Your Health Club Membership."

Your site features health and wellness products. Look at some of the ways to use one tips booklet:

Downloadable bonus - full booklet download for visiting the site, a new title bi-monthly.

1. *Radio/television advertising campaign - "This fitness moment brought to you by (your company's name) Visit www.xyz.com for 109 more great tips like this one."*
2. *Print advertising campaign - a few tips, directing people to your site for more tips.*
3. *Auto responder service - send a tip a day or week, inviting people to your site for more.*
4. *Trade show coupon - offering free downloadable booklet at your web site.*
5. *Product packaging or printed catalog - single tips, directing people to your site.*
6. *Email - a tip within any email from your Customer Service Department or in any electronic invoice, encouraging people to receive more tips when visiting your site.*

Doing this with a different booklet every other month easily broadens your campaign to an entire year, keeping the content fresh, interesting, flowing, and attractive to more traffic. Your next booklets could be:

- *You Can Do It - Walk A Marathon*
- *77 Ways to Prevent and Improve Back Problems*
- *117 Tips for Relieving Arthritis & Muscular Pain*
- *Keep Smiling! 75 Tips for Great Dental Health*
- *108 Ideas for Getting Your Family to Eat Better*

Picture what happens when you translate the same booklet into a different language to reach a non-English speaking population. You can do the same things mentioned here to bring traffic to your site.

Simplify your life and the life of your customers by giving them useful information that will keep them wanting more from you—more information and more of your products.

The article above was reproduced with the permission of Paulette Ensign, and the reader is encouraged to visit her web site www.tipsbooklets.com to get more valuable information about marketing with booklets.

QVC and Home Shopping Network

Periodically, QVC hosts a new product search event around the country. Their web site: http://www.qvcproductsearch.com/ describes these product search programs and where they will be held.

A new product search event is not the only way to submit your product to QVC. Their web site has detailed instructions to submit your product for evaluation. I recommend that you follow these instructions to the letter.

QVC likes products that are very unique and demonstrate very well. They particularly like products that solve a problem in our day-to-day lives or are strongly related to a current subject in the national news.

Another way to get your product on QVC is by way of a sales representative who specializes in placing products on QVC. You can find these reps by reading the business news and trade publications or on QVC itself as sales reps often demonstrate products. You may even be contacted by a QVC rep as a result of the publishing of one of your press releases or from exhibiting in a trade show.

Before you sign with a sales rep, make sure you have a strong contract agreement as many QVC reps command a very high percentage rate. You want to make sure you have a good enough margin because QVC will only consider selling your product for less than it can be bought elsewhere.

Watch the news and the next time you read about a successful entrepreneur who has had their product sold on QVC, contact them. Contact them in the same professional manner that you would with a merchandise buyer. Send a personal letter with your history of sales along with a sample. Follow up the letter with a call in about 2 weeks. Ask them to please evaluate your product for QVC potential; and if they feel your product has merit, ask if they would introduce you to their buyer or contact.

I contacted such an entrepreneur in the manner described in the above paragraph about my product. This person had been the top seller on QVC for the year and happened to live just 45 miles from my home. He loved my product and offered to hand carry it to his buyer.

I was not successful getting my product on QVC. The reason they gave me was, at that time, they believed that our product did not attract a wide enough audience.

The buyer did give us a great marketing idea. She said we should put several of our Clipeze badge holder pins in a gift set in order to reach

the magical price of $15.99. We used this idea and added gift sets containing 4, 5, 6, and 8 pins to our product line.
This gave us over 10 times the margin selling the items individually. We have sold thousands of gifts sets utilizing this suggested marketing idea.

Info-commercials and 30-Direct Response TV

At the writing of this book the economy is at an all time low. One thing that happens in a down economy is that advertisers cut their budgets and do not buy as many TV ads.

This void creates many unsold 30- and 60-second TV spots. Many direct marketers take advantage of the unsold spots and get tremendous prices for them. This means that direct response TV marketers search for new and exciting products to test and to roll out during a slow economy.

One company named TeleBrands, Corp. www.telebrands.com spent an estimated two billion in advertising last year and of that over 300 million was spent on hard selling 30- to 120-second spots.

They usually are paid on a negotiated royalty basis. The preferred method for most of these companies is to contact them by e-mail with facts and pictures of your product.

Exports

Many companies sell their first products overseas by accident. They become what I call accidental exporters.

Exporting is usually a byproduct of your total marketing program. An overseas buyer may first see your product in a catalog, on your web site, or meet you at a trade show here in the US. Others may see your product as a result of your press release being picked up and printed by a newspaper or web news service as they travel on vacation or while in travel in the U.S.

Through web press release services, which are often free, your story can be read around the world.

The best deals and sales will come to you if you conduct proper marketing. If you want to be proactive in going global, the best program I have found is conducted by the US Department of Commerce.

The Department of Commerce has a US Commercial Service program. It is designed to connect you to business opportunities around the world. They have trade specialists based in every US embassy around the world. Their purpose is to introduce US companies to suitable companies in their areas and to act as distributors for US produced products.

The US Commercial Service conducts, sponsors, and participates in many events, such as overseas trade shows, trade missions, and webinars both inside and outside the US.

The fees for the services are reasonable. If you are considering exporting your products, it is advisable to contact your local US commercial service trade specialist. To find the trade specialist near you visit: http://www.buyusa.gov/home/us.html

To find out more about all the programs offered by the US Commercial Service, visit: http://www.buyusa.gov.

A sale to an end user or to a small store or two can basically be like a sale in the US. However, setting up a distributorship is quite different. Business laws vary significantly from country to country. I advise you to consult with an attorney

who specializes in international law before
setting up an overseas distributorship.

The small business developmental center closest
to you should be able to recommend an
international attorney.

Chapter 11

Starting a Business In a Down Economy

You might think that starting a business during down economic times is a bad idea. Many times this is not the case. Some of the largest corporations in the country were started during the Great Depression of the 1930s. Their products, some 70 years later, are still household brand names.

Bad economic times will force you to avoid spending unnecessarily. You should stay in your home office or garage as long as you can and should use basic office furniture and equipment. Most of the equipment you will need is available at thrift stores or garage sales. Computers and printers are often sold during out-of-business sales for steep discounts.

Normal areas to raise money in good times are not available and sometimes this can be a good thing.

Angel investments, venture capital and conventional financing may not be available in down times unless you have discovered a cure for a fatal illness or the common cold. By not borrowing, you can grow in an orderly fashion without large amounts of debt. Remember, I believe in growing slow and steady, and paying as you go and marketing out of earnings.

Buyers of catalogs during slow times are easier to reach by mail and by phone. While they may want to limit the total number of products in their catalog, they must find new products, as new products are the lifeblood of catalogs.

During good economic times, buyers of major catalogs are flooded with new samples. Many times, they simply do not have time to look at them all. During down times, several weeks may go by without a buyer receiving one sample. At the same time, buyers of catalogs are looking for that one product that may make a large difference in sales during the next catalog run and possibly save their company from future financial problems.

During such times, prototype makers and product manufacturers are more receptive to new lines as well. Many manufacturers lose product lines from companies that go out of business. This creates openings. They are also more willing to do smaller runs at lower prices in the economy we are now experiencing.

Mail volume decreases as postage rates increase and companies cut back on mail marketing. When a potential customer receives less mail, they are more likely to see and open well-targeted direct mail pieces. This lifts response rates. Printers have too much down time on their presses and will negotiate and do short runs.

Magazines are more likely to negotiate for space ads, allowing you to receive deep discounts during down times. Even press releases to newspapers and magazines are easier to get published as reporters and editors have less staff and time to go looking for stores. Many times, a well-written press release will be inserted directly as you sent it at the very last second to fill space in order to make a deadline.

The importance of trade shows was discussed in previous chapters. During slow times, fewer buyers travel to trade shows, but the buyers who do attend have added pressure on them to find new and exciting products to bring back to their superiors to justify the expense of attending shows. Also, you will have fewer exhibitors to compete with for the buyer's attention due to the fact that companies that exhibit will limit the shows they travel to during a slow economy.

Trade show promoters are much more likely to negotiate for sponsorships and advertising opportunities during a down economy.

In a down economy, it is even more important that you keep your day job until you have at least one year's pay in the bank. It is also important to do your utmost not to incur debt.

Chapter 12

Negotiating

Negotiation is extremely important in running a business. I advise you to read several books on the subject.

Most businesses that sell both retail and wholesale have a price structure something like the one described below:

- **Full Retail Price**
  This price is the full price charged for a product. An example of this is, the sticker price for an automobile at a dealership.

  Most people do not pay this price, but once in a while an inexperienced customer will. Another reason to have a full retail price is to protect your dealers or resellers who may be able to discount this price and still make a good margin.

This price also gives you a good basis to discount during customer negotiating. It also is important when and if you donate some of your products as a charitable contribution to a worthy cause.

- **Discounted Retail Price or On Sale Price**
This is a price that retail customers get with little or no negotiating and/or during a special sale.

- **Wholesale Prices**: This is the price for dealers or your resellers. This is for small or average size dealers, such as retail stores.

- **Discounted Wholesale Prices**: This price is for the best and largest resellers. Many times this is the price that would be quoted if you were negotiating with very large catalogs. Catalogs mail to thousands and sometimes millions of customers. They are distributor and retailer rolled into one.

- **The Family Price**: This is the price that an owner gives to family and close friends. This price does not make money but they do not lose money either. They do benefit from the word of mouth advertising that comes along with this type of purchase.

Many experienced buyers who work for major retail chains or large catalogs are more than aware of this kind of price structure. Often times a business will be requested to provide a total cost breakdown.

The business will be asked to provide a price for 100, 500, 1,000, 10,000 or more units. Obviously the price for 10,000 units is the discounted wholesale price. It is advisable to stick with your price structure and determine how many units equal what price as many will offer to buy say 100 units but want the 10,000-unit price.

Remember a steadfast rule in negotiations: if you give up something you should get something in return. In the previous paragraph, say the buyer of a larger catalog wants to buy 100 units but only wants to pay the 10,000 unit price. You feel that the 100 units might lead to thousands of unit sales in the future. You might agree to the price but only if they prepay all their orders by credit card before shipment.

When you are on the buying end with suppliers and vendors, remember that you want a good price, but you want a fair price. If you want to start a long-term relationship with a manufacturer/accountant, etc., the price you pay needs to be enough for them to make a fair margin to give you the best and reliable service. If one side or the other feels that they are not getting a good deal, service will suffer.

It is more than okay to shop around for a good deal, but keep in mind a new manufacturer or service provider will almost always undercut a current supplier to obtain your business. Once the new supplier gets your business, only time will show if they will provide good and reliable service.

I want to share with you a simple and fast strategy I have learned to get better prices on just about everything. This is great both for business and in your personal life. First, ask for the price of an item even if the product is marked with a price tag. Upon getting the price give a FLINCH followed by, "You will need to do better than that." You will be surprised when doing this how often the seller will immediately reduce the asking price of the item. And yes, you can even FLINCH over the phone. I have done this many times and I am amazed at how often it works.

A win-win result is much better than a win-lose

result, particularly when you are trying to form a joint venture. Keep in mind the following points when negotiating an important or critical business matter:

- You must be prepared. Find out as much as you can about the party you are negotiating with before you sit down with them.
- Make sure you know all your facts about your goals and make sure you know all the issues before making any compromises.
- Make sure you understand all legal and or tax consequences that may result in an agreement between parties. Analyze counterpart's position and anticipate the goals they hope to accomplish. You need to prepare alternatives to make it possible to reach their objectives in a way both parties can benefit.
- Always be truthful. If both parties are not truthful, confidence will be lost and the agreement will not happen. Telling the truth, even if it is not good news, will earn trust and confidence. Keep in mind that if false information is given and a deal is struck, you leave your company open to legal

problems in the future.

- Respect the other party. If you are cordial, you may be able to gain information that you would not be able to during stressful negotiations. If you determine that an agreement will not happen, it is still to your advantage to respect the other party. You never know what the future will bring and you may find yourself facing them in the future. As the saying goes, "Don't burn your bridges".

- Try to be sure the party you are negotiating with has the authority to make the decision. It is very common to hammer out a great compromise only to find out that the other party does not have the authority to make the decision and has to report back to their management. This is very common strategy and can be frustrating.

- Observe and listen to the other party intensely. Often a key word or expression can reveal the true goal of the other party. Pay attention to body language. As one of the other party speaks, the second member may have a revealing contradictory expression.

- The person who needs the deal the most is at a big disadvantage. If you need the deal the most, do not let the other party know it. Most of the time, the party that needs the deal the most will compromise first. They will make concessions time and time again, while the company that does not need the deal will have to concede very little or not at all.
- Keep your emotions in check. You need to be prepared to calmly walk away if the deal does not meet your needs. A bad deal is much worse than no deal. You want to guard against being so emotional that you make a deal you will regret later.
- If you deal in person, always look the other party in the eye. Do not waiver.

Most day-to-day negotiations are informal. Many will be with your buyers and vendors. Always try to concentrate on common ground that benefits both companies.

One of my first catalog customers called me before our products appeared the first time in their catalog. They had ordered 58 units of our product and their catalog mailing date had been pushed back a few weeks. They wanted to know if I would take half the units back.

The catalog was on a net 30-payment schedule but their catalog mailing date was in about 45 days. I suggested that we increase the payment terms to net 60 for this order. This way they would not have to pay until their catalog had been mailed out. We had shipped several thousand units to retail stores across the US and I had little doubt that this catalog would sell a thousand times more than the initial order of 58, but this made them feel at ease.

We ended up selling over 150,000 CLIPEZE to this company over the six-month period of that catalog run. The buyer and I still joke about them asking to return half of those 58 units.

Chapter 13

Business Phases and Cycles

The idea of business cycles is not new. Joseph A. Schumpeter is credited with the concept. He wrote *Theory of Economic Development* (1911), where he first outlined his famous theory of entrepreneurship. His four phases were called: boom, recession, depression and recovery.

In modern times some have referred to business cycles, such as boom, greed, fear and bust.

All companies go though phases and cycles. The phases below are what I experienced and have knowledge of for a home-based startup business. Because you have just started with your idea or business, you may ask why this is important now. Knowledge of phases is very helpful for successful planning for growth for both business and personal goals.

Trial Phase

In this phase, the idea, product or service, is tested to see if it is marketable and to see if the product can be produced at a profit. During this phase, the niches will be identified for direct marketing. A prototype is developed and tested.

Start-up Phase

During this phase, the company structure, such as a C corporation, or sole proprietor, is set up. Manufacturing of your product is started.

Initial sales begin from direct marketing catalogs or other outlets, giving you a residual income for start-up cost. Your web site and credit card processing system are created. Press releases will open doors and expand your business.

Growth Phase

As the sales of your product grow you will be able to expand into other catalogs and into retail stores. Growth in this phase can happen very fast. You may sign up sales representatives and exhibit in several trade shows. The result may be exploding sales during this phase. Try to resist incurring debt as you race to keep up with demand for your product.

You will build up inventories and more than likely move into commercial space. You have a high demand for suppliers in several areas such as printing product catalogs, office and shipping supplies, etc. At this time, banks are willing to lend as they read about and witness your success. In this phase you usually hire employees and the demand for your product can justify increasing prices. You may have shortages of product due to demand by customers.

Leveling Off or Maturity Phase

Your catalog customers and your resellers order on a regular basis and you will have a steady stream of web or retail sales direct to your end user. Expenses and taxes increase during this phase. You may have reached product saturation and possibly have become a well-know brand in your industry. Competitors are, at this point, copying your product or coming out with more innovative designs or products that compete with your products. Unsold inventory starts to build up. Guard against wastefulness during this phase. Employees may view the success of the company as an opportunity to ask for merit raises

Decline or Slow Decline Phase

It does not matter if you are a small "mom and pop" organization or Microsoft®. A company will go into a gradual or steep decline after a period of time. This has to do with several factors in our capitalist system.

Companies in this phase often lose thousands, even millions of dollars, due to product knock-offs. Costs associated with payroll and utilities add to overhead. Sometimes price increases in raw materials over time make a product unprofitable.

There is also a hard-to-explain phenomenon in this country. People love the underdog. They do love to see a small guy succeed, but they also love to tear down the large industrial giant or market leader. At times, jealousy comes into play.

Knowing these phases as you start your business is very helpful in planning. As you develop your ideas and start to be successful, you need to keep these phases in mind. They can help you manage success and guard against the false notion that your company will just grow, grow and grow without a downturn.

Many entrepreneurs decide to sell their businesses during the growth or leveling off phase. Some decide starting businesses is their specialty, not running them. Others decide that running businesses and taking them to the next level is what they do best. Still others are successful building a small business into a Fortune 500 company.

Some people are gifted and can do it all, but most of the time people who have successful start-ups have a difficult time running a mid-to-large sized business. It takes a different set of skills to take a small business to the next level and become a successful large business. Dealing with employees, taxes, outside investors, and other circumstances can pose quite a challenge for an entrepreneur.

Some multinational corporations can counter or disrupt the business cycle by merging or acquiring other companies. This way they do business between companies and become their own largest customers. Many very large companies acquire up to 30 or more companies a year to counter the business phases.

Chapter 14

Persistence, Commitment And Integrity

Persistence and commitment are the keys to success. As everyone knows, most small businesses fail. It is my opinion, based on my experience, that most fail due to lack of effort or lack of persistence.

If you work hard, have an outstanding product, and provide great customer service, your chances of being successful improve substantially.

Certainly outside events can adversely influence your start-up business, such as family illnesses, natural disasters, etc. These are things you do not have control over but you can overcome if you follow these simple guidelines.

You need to do what you say you are going to do. Later on, if you have employees, you need to make sure they are following your lead, doing what they told the customer they would do. It sounds simple, but you would be surprised how many people will tell you one thing and do another. For example if you say the product is shipping out today, make sure it does.

Early in my business, before most of our customers started ordering regularly, I would have customers call me late in the day and want an order sent overnight because they forgot to order for a special event. Many times, they would call after our freight carrier made their pickup. I would get in my car and drive 25 miles to the carrier's headquarters even for only a $25 order, despite the fact that that was the last thing I wanted to do after working my day job all day.

I received countless calls from grateful customers. But better still, these customers often became large, repeat customers. A commitment needs to be made that your business will not fail due to lack of effort.

I strongly advise that you set up and run your business using the highest ethical standards. You need to learn and adhere to tax regulations from the very start of your business. The IRS has valuable information on their web site: www.irs.gov.

Do not engage in unethical business practices. I have been told of those who give kickbacks or expensive gifts to buyers for their business. They always lose in the end. Your company needs to be true to its word. It should be your company policy to always be truthful with customers, vendors and employees.

In the national news, as this book is being written, many business owners who have been unethical are being caught and arrested. In some cases, owners have had Chinese manufacturers send invoices with higher amounts than the products actually cost. The manufacturer keeps the actual price and then wires the excess amounts to individual offshore bank accounts where the income and interest is not reported to the IRS. These individuals now face stiff fines and possible jail time as the US government is pursuing them.

Dealing with Catalog and Store Buyers

After your trial period, you may very well feel your first frustration trying to get the attention of a catalog or store buyer.

It is very important that you be persistent in your pursuit of them. Buyers are busy people and many will not take or return phone calls readily. For reasons I cannot explain, personnel on the buying end of a transaction sometimes feel they do not have the responsibility to return phone calls, faxes or e-mail.

Catalog buyers, however, may call you when they need something at any hour and ask you to deliver products or samples overnight. Often this is because they work around deadlines for such things as product photo shoots. I advise you to be ready for this, because if you are ready, it can make the difference in getting your product into a catalog.

When you can get samples to them quickly, it can get your product into a catalog. If a catalog buyer with a tight deadline needs a product that is available from two different sources, he will use the one that consistently provides what he needs the fastest.

Keep in mind that today's junior buyer may become tomorrow's senior buyer or even VP of marketing. Business is all about relationships.

Most buyers use e-mail as the preferred method for communication. Often, this is because they can receive and send e-mail when they are out of the office.

Be prepared to leave a voice mail message if you call them. I often call a new buyer by phone and leave a message informing them that I will be sending them e-mail. This helps them to recognize your e-mail in the large volumes of e-mail they receive. Make sure you put something in the subject line that the buyer will recognize like, "Follow up for submitted samples," or, "I met you at the trade show."

Always be personable with the buyers you come in contact with. Often they like doing business with small companies. When asked, buyers can offer good product advice and even new ideas for products. I will regularly ask them if there is any product they would like to see out in the marketplace. Additionally, I ask them if they have any demands by their customers that are not being met.

I make time in my schedule to send letters and samples on certain days of the week and to follow up on another day of the week.

Dealing with Mistakes

We all make mistakes. The old saying, "Show me a person who does not make mistakes and I will show you a person who doesn't do anything," is certainly true. You will make mistakes along your journey. The key is to make small mistakes, not large ones. It sounds easy, but it is not. Your company can recover from several small mistakes, but one large one can put you out of business.

There are several steps you can take to cut down on mistakes and problems. One key in avoiding large mistakes that can doom your company is to choose your business associates very carefully. I mentioned early in this book how important it is to get and check references for people and companies that you do business with.

You always want to make sure you have a written and signed contract for important services, such as product manufacturing. A competent business attorney should prepare these contracts.

If the party is a small entity, make sure the principal of the company signs a personal guarantee. A personal guarantee holds the individual liable, along with their company, for damages if something goes wrong.

It is advisable to insist that a company has sufficient insurance in case product liability or defect problems should occur. Require that your manufacturers or large vendors provide a letter from their insurance company. Always CHECK

IT by calling and confirming the coverage with the insurance company directly.

I go to the search engine Google and search for every company and person I consider doing business with. It only takes a minute and it is amazing what you can find out about a person or company just by typing in their name.

As I write this paragraph, I just put my own name in Google and came up with over 500 results. I then Googled CLIPEZE, my product name, and received 7500 results.

A business associate introduced me to a man who wanted to meet with me about a distributorship to a chain of discount stores. We had a very good meeting in my office and as he walked out of my office into the parking lot, I put his name in Google.

There were hundreds of results. None of the results were about his claimed business experience. What I found was the fact he was a proclaimed atheist and was the leader of several atheist clubs in a nearby large city. Whether or not this man was an atheist would not influence my willingness to do business with him, however, some of the links showed him leading many demonstrations holding explicit offensive signs.

You should know as much as you can about a person before you sign a contract with him or her to do business. Many times you must trust your own judgment for staying out of trouble.

Once during a trade show in New York, a man motioned me to the side of my booth to talk privately. He asked if I could give him a price for a 100,000-piece custom CLIPEZE badge holder to be bought by and shipped to the country of Iran. I told him that I understood that US companies are prohibited from trading with Iran. He said that it did not matter because they had a company in France, which could act as a go-between. I took his business card, but as he walked away I had imagined the possible outcomes of doing business with him. One vision I had included the evening news showing a violent demonstration by radical extremist burning an American Flag. As the camera panned the demonstrators, I imagined all of them were wearing CLIPEZE badge holders. I tossed his card in the trash. Keep your business dealings ethical.

Remember, the key to your business is steady growth. Start small and grow at a manageable rate. Just like a child, your company needs to learn to crawl before it can walk and walk before it can run.

Getting your product placed in a large retail chain such as Wal-Mart® sounds wonderful, but it could be devastating to a new business. Wal-Mart® and several other large retail chains require you to use Electric Data Interchange (EDI). EDI is very complicated and expensive to set up. It involves the setting up of labels compatible with the retailers scanning system at their warehouses or distribution centers. To become EDI qualified often you must hire a vendor company to handle the process.

When using EDI, if packaging is not correct or is misread by the scanner, the manufacturer is charged a fee per affected carton. This fee is deducted by electronic debit from your bank account.

Large retail chains often order large quantities of merchandise with short delivery times. This is very dangerous for a new, small company.

Always remember that it is very dangerous to rely on a single customer for 40% or more of your total business.

I know of a person who, after just six months in business, landed a huge retail chain as a customer. He celebrated. The company was able to borrow the large amount of money he needed for the enormous first order and the EDI system. He already had a manufacturer in Asia for his products.
Everything went well and the large first order was shipped ahead of schedule.

When the container ship approached the docks, disaster struck. In California, the Longshoreman's Union went on a labor strike over wages and refused to unload any container ships.

All the ships had to wait offshore in order of arrival. This caused his products to be very late. Even though he had a good reason, the cancel date on the purchase order had expired and the buyer called and canceled the order.

His company was responsible to the bank to repay his debt and no longer had a buyer for the containers full of his products. Later, much later, the same retail chain made him an offer to buy the products below cost.

Remember, in order to build a tall skyscraper, you first need to have a deep, strong and solid foundation.

If you follow the recommendations of this book you will keep your day job, and will first sell during your trial period to family, friends and others around you. Second, you will sell to a catalog or two, and then on to retail sales through your web site or from the benefits of several press releases. You then will be ready to branch out to small retail stores through sales representatives. Then and only then are some businesses ready to sell to large retail chains.

It takes a lot of courage to turn down a large retail chain when your company is not ready to serve them. It is better to turn down business than to make promises you are unable to fulfill.

Product Quality and Liability

Product quality and liability are the most frequent source of major problems.

My second product was called CLOGEZE Shoes. I got the idea to silk-screen artwork in our CLIPEZE art library onto clog type shoes for the medical industry.

I wanted to mimic what had been done with scrubs (the clothes medical personnel wear). Scrubs started in only white or blue. Today they have colorful prints and hundreds of colors and patterns. I thought this could be done with the plain white professional shoes that are worn by medical personnel. CLOGEZE Shoes became an instant success.

Just by sending some samples to JC Penney in Dallas, Texas, we were able to get them in the JC Penney Uniform Catalog. The first order was for over $38,000 worth of product. Based on that sale, I also placed CLOGEZE Shoes into the largest catalog in Canada, which placed another very large first order of over $20,000. Then additional catalogs that carried our other products began to order CLOGEZE.

Despite asking for and then checking references of the manufacturer and the US representative for quality control, I ran into major problems. I first bought one container of shoes, approximately 7,000 pairs. We quickly sold all of them. I ordered 2 more containers. The manufacturer in China wanted to make it three more containers because it would be cheaper to manufacture them all at once.

We got a good price and bought the 3rd. Just days after wiring over $300,000 to the Asian manufacturer, I started getting phone calls from customers. At first, I received one or two each day. The volume increased until I was fielding dozens of calls each day. All the calls were the same. The heels on the shoes were cracking.

I sued the US company, which had failed to perform the quality test as specified in our contract. We won a $755,000 dollar judgment. As of yet we have been unable to collect even one penny of the judgment from the limited liability company. The loss still affects me today.

I should have stayed with the original order of one container. It is okay to run completely out of stock of a product. I checked the quality company's reference, but I did not have them sign a personal guarantee nor did I carry an insurance policy. I did not follow my own advice, and it cost me a lot of money. You can benefit from my mistake. Be careful! The correct action for me to have followed was to have gone slower.

Always, I mean always, inspect and count your shipments yourself. For the first year or two, do not delegate this job to anyone else. When you grow to the point that you let employees do this job for you, it is advisable to spot-check your products regularly.

We have an epidemic in this country of poor quality products being produced in Asia and shipped to small companies. Only when poor quality products affect large companies, such as human or pet food sources, have they reached the news media. Be advised that the US government will not help you with quality problems from Asia, at least in my experience they haven't.

The best defense for quality problems is to build a strong relationship with a manufacturer either in the USA or abroad. I said early in this book, and I think needs to be repeated, it is important to always have more than one manufacturer.

Chapter 15

Does Money Change You?

I do not believe money changes you, however, it certainly changes the people around you. Use purchase orders and contractor agreement contracts from the start of your business.

Purchase orders can be created out of any accounting software program such as QuickBooks® or Peachtree®. A purchase order is a written authorization for goods and services, specifying the price and terms of payment. This is a legally binding contract once accepted by both parties.

I would advise to use this method for all expenses unless you are using a company credit card for items like hotel room, tradeshow reservations, etc.

Make sure you use a purchase order for the manufacture of your product.

Remember, you are a boss or business owner first. Personal relationships can easily cloud your judgment when you are inexperienced.

When I was away exhibiting in almost monthly trade shows, I delegated the responsibility to order office and shipping supplies to a trusted employee. I found out later that the supply companies often offer gifts for certain levels of purchases. As a result, the employee would order $150.00 worth of supplies when we needed much less in order to receive a free small TV, radio or such. Employees left unchecked often will spend a lot of your hard-earned money. Months after discovering this ordering scheme, I still have enough pens and other supplies to last me for years to come.

When you hire an independent contractor, be sure you prepare and have a signed contractor agreement. If you do not have such an agreement in place you may not own the material produced by the contractor.

This applies to such items as your web site, brochure, photos of your product, and even your company logo. I advise you to read the information at www.nolo.com to ensure you acquire the details you should know.

On the search engines, such as Google, you can find examples to download free for use simply by typing the terms *work for hire* and *contractor agreement contract.* I also advise you to use a purchase order with all the terms clearly spelled out. In the case of graphic artwork, make sure you have a disk of all artwork delivered to you before payment. Always specify that your company will own all rights to the material produced under the agreement.

It is advisable to file copyright protection on your company logo and other important artwork, as discussed earlier in the book.

When some accountants, lawyers, and graphic designers, etc., see money coming in, you may experience a sudden increase in their fees for services rendered. You need to guard against this no matter how well you think you know them or how long you have been doing business with them.

Employees

Problems and employees go hand and hand. It is my advice to do without employees as long as you can except for perhaps one assistant or someone to help you ship or take orders.

I worked my day job and ran my business for almost 2 years. My routine was to stop at the post office on my way home every afternoon. I would return calls and invoice orders when I got home. I packed orders late at night before going to bed.

About the time we signed up sales representatives and they started placing our products into about 100 new stores a month, fulfilling our orders became a lot for one person to handle. My wife helped me when she could, but she had a full-time job. She undertook the routine household requirements that previously we both had shared which gave me a lot of relief.

Many nights, I was still in my work uniform when my wife would surprise me by bringing dinner into my home office at 7:00 pm. Often, I was in my office working until 11:30pm. Then, I was up at 4:15am to check and answer e-mail.

One morning before work, my wife and I were sharing a cup of coffee and looking at a stack of priority boxes on our kitchen table. The pile went almost to the ceiling. We looked at each other and said at the same instant, "I think we need to hire someone."

My first employee was named Kay. She was a wonderful lady and made my life so much easier. She had just retired but needed a part time job to help her with expenses. From that point on, I did the selling, marketing, invoicing, etc., and Kay handled all the packing and shipping. Neither one of us had any business experience, but we learned together.

Chapter 16

Customer Service

Customer service is extremely important. Obviously without sales to customers, your business will not exist.

Keep track of all your customers from the very beginning. Use the customer relationship marketing (CRM) function of your e-mail program to keep records of your customers. There you can make notes and list special information to help with future sales. Your customer list is a very valuable asset for your company.

Remember, the person most likely to buy from you in the future is the person who has just bought from you. This is because they are satisfied with their purchase. They will tell others and probably will decide to give your product as gifts to family and friends. More than likely, they are receiving compliments and being asked where they purchased the unique product.

You should study CRM. There are many great books on the subject, including books by Lois Geller listed in the reference section of this book. She is an authority on CRM.

CRM: What Does It Mean?
Lois Geller wrote the article below. It is reproduced here with her permission.

I am a shopper. And I buy from many companies in their stores, on their web sites, through direct mail and from catalogs. I buy cosmetics online from Sephora.com, airline tickets from Expedia.com, books and music from Amazon.com, and clothes from Lord and Taylor and Loehmann's.

But honestly, other than Amazon and Loehmann's, few companies do anything but take my money and deliver the goods. They almost never make the extra effort to develop a relationship with me—or as Ford Motor Co. puts it, "surprise and delight" me in any way. You may ask: "Why would they want to build a relationship with me?" For starters, it'll help them keep me as a customer, and if they keep customers, they won't have to spend as much money acquiring new *ones. When you think about the lifetime value (LTV) of a single customer, it's a wonder more companies don't bend over backwards to keep customers happy.*

I buy airline tickets through Expedia.com, because every few weeks I visit my mother in Florida. And yet Expedia has never e-mailed me an offer for Florida. It sends me e-mails offering 15-percent off Quantas to Australia, but no great offers to Florida.

When I talk to potential clients about retention CRM, the objection I usually get is: "Why should we spend money on current customers? They're already buying from us." Here's why: If you don't offer your customers something special— something that's of real value, that's relevant— when another company does make that offer, they'll leave you.

One company makes a serious effort to build a relationship with me: Franklin Covey. I once took a course on organizing my life with the Franklin Covey method. Not only did I get my schedule and life on track, but I also got a chance to see Covey's CRM operation in action.

After I took the course, it gave me a gift certificate to go to its Rockefeller Center store to pick any size planner that fit my needs. That definitely got the relationship off to a good start! I was so interested in its approach that I called Eric Bright, Covey's director of catalog marketing. Following are some of the things he told me about how Covey gets up close and cozy with its customers and builds loyalty:

What Customers Need

CRM is not about the software or some million-dollar technology—it must start with looking at needs, specifically what customers need.

Recently I ordered pantyhose, and I got an e-mail confirmation almost immediately. Sure, it's a step in the right direction, but it's just the first step. When it comes to communicating with customers across channels, there are many disconnects. It seems that the technology still isn't smart enough. Most business owners who have been around a while seem to be smarter than the smartest technology, better at offering customers what they want and showing customers how much they value them.

Some of the challenges we face include: There are few loyalty clubs in multi-channel environments, but unifying loyalty programs across channels should be a big deal. Limited

Too and other companies work to deliver this for their best customers.

I believe CRM will work. Often it seems that interactions have occurred in silos. When and if you create meaningful conversations through flexible systems that bridge different environments, you'll be effective.

Companies such as Amazon.com, eBags.com and Franklin Covey use CRM to meet and anticipate customer needs, and are leading the way. Software itself can accomplish many things. It can make business move faster and help you see relationships you might have missed. It can remind you to follow up. But too many companies are asking technology to do the one thing it really can't do: manage a relationship.

CRM has a chance of working once companies recognize that it doesn't exist separate from the business strategies and processes of a company. Success requires planning, and a rush to adopt technology without strategy is dangerous. Software is only a means to an end.

For CRM to succeed, there must be a strategy in place that makes sense. And there must be people in place who have direct marketing sensibilities.

I dream that one day when I buy from nearly any retail store, I'll also be given information about service online. I'll be able to buy from a store and return the item to a central distribution center and get credit on my card. I'll even get appropriate offers based on prior purchases and preferences. A company will thank me for my purchases—recognize me when I call. And it will know when I've defected and invite me to come back. Then I will be a loyal customer forever.

LOIS K. GELLER is president of Lois Geller Marketing Group, a full-service direct response agency in Hollywood, Florida. She is the author of *RESPONSE! The Complete Guide to Profitable Direct Marketing* and *Customers for Keeps*, published in 2002. Visit www.loisgellermarketinggroup.com or e-mail lois@loisgellermarketinggroup.com

Other CRM Ideas
The book *80/20 Principle* by Richard Koch is listed in the reference section also and offers great insights to customer behavior. I have found a lot of truth to the teachings of this book that 80% of our revenue comes from 20% of our customers. Mr. Koch provides great advice as to how to spend your time and marketing dollars to get the best returns.

I advise you to stay in contact with your established customers. Contact them at least monthly. The most cost-efficient way to contact them is by e-mail. Get as much information when they order as you can, including their e-mail address. It is a good idea to contact them after the sale and offer a discount on their next purchase.

Additionally, consider sending your customers evaluation forms for their opinions and suggestions. Sometimes they offer great ways to improve your product or even offer related new product ideas to you for free. On these forms, ask them for some personal information, but give the option to leave blanks if they want to do so. If they provide personal information, such as their birth date, send them a discount offer every year in their birth month. Involve them in some design decisions, if possible.

Let your customers feel like they are a part of your sales force. This can result in the best advertising you can get, word of mouth.

E-mail them with give-away specials. Send them an e-mail version of press releases or announcements. Inform them about new places where your product will be sold. Or, just send an e-mail to thank them for buying your product.

When you first start out with your business, you may only have five or ten customers, but find out about them, keep the information in a database, and contact them often.

Customer service does not have to be complicated. Simply treat your customers as you would want to be treated when you make a purchase. When dealing with mad or irate customers, I often say first and foremost I am sorry for our error. I tell the customer that we will be more than happy to correct our mistake if they will allow us to do so.

Then I proceed to take the action required to make things right. This satisfies the overwhelming majority of unhappy customers. I cannot tell you how many times I have resolved a problem for a customer and, while still on the phone, I made a new sale to the now satisfied customer. Don't get me wrong. There will be rare customers who are totally unreasonable, and you will not satisfy them; but, do your best and be fair to them.

Chapter 17

Rewards of Owning Your Own Business

Being in business for yourself and bringing a unique product to market can be very rewarding. You get to be your own boss and create your own future. You make your own decisions. You set your own hours.

A recurring issue in today's workplace is that a few hard workers often have to carry the entire workload. Many times they have to make up for slackers who are allowed to skate by doing only minimal work. Often this creates a situation where unqualified and undeserving employees are often promoted into supervisory positions, creating a very stressful work environment.

You can escape from this environment. If you work hard and are successful at your own business, you will benefit. You can enrich the lives of your family, employees, vendors and customers.

It is a wonderful feeling to create wealth from an idea that just came to you. You can touch lives from 7,000 miles away to the business next door.

The success of your business reaches people and places that you may not think of. One day, I was at my desk in my office when the intercom buzzed. One of my employees told me that a lady was on the phone. She was a customer of ours who owned a retail store in the Midwest.

She wanted to talk to me to let me know that her store had been destroyed by fire. I took the call and the lady explained that she had lost her building and all the contents. She said that everything was fully insured and she would be able to pay her bill, but that there was going to be a delay. I told her that the time delay was fine and for her to take as much time as she needed. I wished her well and the conversation ended.

As I hung up the phone I brought up her customer history. She was a very good long-term customer. I buzzed my employee. I told her to zero out the invoice for this customer and to send her a replacement order with the items on her last order. I also wrote a note to let her know that the pending order would be taken care of and the replacement order would also be free, and we wished her the best of luck. I went back to my work and soon forgot the event. About two years later, we were exhibiting in a large trade show with over three-thousand attendees and hundreds of exhibitors in a large city. We had a crowd of about 25-retail storeowners in front of our booth. An employee and I were giving our sales speeches, handing out samples and collecting contact information.

Suddenly, a woman came around to the back of the table and proceeded to give me a long embrace. She looked at me with tears in her eyes and said she wanted to thank me so much for what I had done.

She then turned to the crowd in front of our booth and proceeded to tell them how our company had helped her after her store had burned down. It was at that moment that I realized how much of an impact owning a business has on all people you come in contact with.

Remember, you are not just starting a business, you are extending your idea, your creation, into the world. You will never know the impact your product makes on everyone in the world. But you will make a difference, to many, whether large or small. Make the best choices you can make. As a business owner, you will leave a mark on your community.

Being a business owner gives you a platform to operate from. It gives you a voice to be heard. In our society, opinions of presidents, CEOs, and business owners influence others or generate great interest. Business owners help make a community what it is. It is a great responsibility. Use it wisely.

Appendix 1

Provisional Patent

The text below is found on the US Patent Office web site and describes the Provisional Patent in detail. Go to http://www.uspto.gov/web/offices/pac/provapp.htm for more information.

Since June 8, 1995, the United States Patent and Trademark Office (USPTO) has offered inventors the option of filing a provisional application for patent which was designed to provide a lower-cost first patent filing in the United States.

Applicants are entitled to claim the benefit of a provisional application in a corresponding non-provisional application filed not later than 12 months after the provisional application filing date.

Under the provisions of 35 U.S.C. § 119(e), the corresponding non-provisional application would benefit in three ways: (1) patent ability would be evaluated as though filed on the earlier provisional application filing date, (2) the resulting publication or patent would be treated as a reference under 35 U.S.C. § 102(e) as of the earlier provisional application filing date, and (3) the twenty-year patent term would be measured from the later non-provisional application filing date. Thus, domestic applicants are placed on equal footing with foreign applicants with respect to the patent term. Inventors may file U.S. provisional applications regardless of citizenship. Note that provisional applications cannot claim the benefit of a previously filed application, either foreign or domestic. Note also that 35 U.S.C. § 112 must be complied with as discussed in the paragraph below in order to receive the benefit under 35 U.S.C. § 119(e).

The later-filed non-provisional application claiming the benefit of the provisional application must include at least one claim particularly pointing out and distinctly claiming the subject matter, which the applicant regards as the invention. **See** 35 U.S.C. § 112, 2nd paragraph. Although a claim is not required in a provisional application, the written description and any drawing(s) of the provisional application must adequately support the subject matter claimed in the later-filed non-provisional application in order for the later-filed non-provisional application to benefit from the provisional application filing date.

Therefore, care should be taken to ensure that the disclosure filed as the provisional application adequately provides a written description of the full scope of the subject matter regarded as the invention and desired to be claimed in the later filed non-provisional application.

There is no requirement that the written description and any drawings filed in a provisional application and a later-filed non-provisional application be identical, however, the later-filed non-provisional application is only entitled to the benefit of the common subject matter disclosed in the corresponding non-provisional application filed not later than 12 months after the provisional application filing date.

Additionally the specification shall disclose the manner and process of making and using the invention, in such full, clear, concise and exact terms as to enable any person skilled in the art to which the invention pertains to make and use the invention and set forth the best mode

contemplated for carrying out the invention.
See 35 U.S.C. § 112, 1st paragraph

A provisional application for patent is a U. S.
national application for patent filed in the
USPTO under 35 U.S.C. § 111(b). It allows filing
without a formal patent claim, oath or
declaration, or any information disclosure (prior
art) statement. It provides the means to
establish an early effective filing date in a later-
filed non-provisional patent application filed
under 35 U.S.C. § 111(a). It also allows the term
"Patent Pending" to be applied in connection
with the description of the invention.

A provisional application for patent (provisional
application) has a pendency lasting 12 months
from the date the provisional application is
filed. The 12-month pendency period cannot be
extended. Therefore, an applicant who files a
provisional application must file a
corresponding non-provisional application for
patent (non-provisional application) during the
12-month pendency period of the provisional
application in order to benefit from the earlier
filing of the provisional application. In
accordance with 35 U.S.C. § 119(e), the
corresponding non-provisional application must
contain or be amended to contain a specific
reference to the provisional application within

the time period and in the manner required by 37 CFR 1.78.

Once a provisional application is filed, an alternative to filing a corresponding non-provisional application is to convert the provisional application to a non-provisional application by filing a grantable petition under 37 CFR § 1.53(c)(3) requesting such a conversion within 12 months of the provisional application filing date.

However, converting a provisional application to a non-provisional application (versus filing a non-provisional application claiming the benefit of the provisional application) will have a negative impact on patent term. The term of a patent issuing from a non-provisional application resulting from the conversion of a provisional application will be measured from the original filing date of the provisional application.

By filing a provisional application first, and then filing a corresponding non-provisional application that references the provisional application within the 12-month provisional application pendency period, a patent term endpoint may be extended by as much as 12 months.

Provisional Application for Patent Filing Date Requirements

The provisional application must be made in the name(s) of all of the inventor(s). It can be filed up to 12 months following the date of first sale, offer for sale, public use, or publication of the invention. (These pre-filing disclosures, although protected in the United States, may preclude patenting in foreign countries.)

A filing date will be accorded to a provisional application only when it contains: a written description of the invention, complying with all requirements of 35 U.S.C. §112 1st paragraph and any drawings necessary to understand the invention, complying with 35 U.S.C. §113.

If either of these items are missing or incomplete, no filing date will be accorded to the provisional application.

To be complete, a provisional application must also include the filing fee and a cover sheet identifying:

- the application as a provisional application for patent;
- the name(s) of all inventors;
- inventor residence(s);

- title of the invention;
- name and registration number of the attorney or agent and docket number (if applicable);
- correspondence address; and
- any US government agency that has a property interest in the application.

Appendix 2

Testing Direct Mail

This Appendix contains a copy of a white paper reproduced with permission written by Robert Dunhill, President of Dunhill International List Co.

It still amazes me, after nearly 50 years in direct marketing, how few companies understand and actually do enough direct market testing.

The only logical explanation is that test is a four-letter word. And people don't like to use four letter words, right?

From a direct marketing standpoint, we can test the list(s), the offer, the package creative, and components of the package, the format, and so on.

The ability to test and measure results is what differentiates direct marketing from all other communications efforts. Testing, when done correctly, will help a company decrease the number of pieces mailed and intentionally increase its return-on-investment (ROI).

Testing allows us to determine, in a real world setting, what works, what doesn't work and why. Like direct marketing itself, testing is only about numbers, ROI and data.

A grid or matrix allows the direct mailer to test and track several lists, creative approaches and offers at once.

My advice is to set-up a testing matrix and test within budget parameters. The goal is to break even or make money on your testing while simultaneously learning as much as possible. A word of caution though ~ make sure that the test cells implemented are meaningful. If they are not, you will waste money. For instance, testing outer envelope teaser copy seldom produces significant lifts in response rates.

Testing does not have to be complicated.

The practice of testing involves simple techniques to collect data. Data in turn becomes knowledge, which you need to succeed, move forward and grow.

Testing is a progressive art and can help make marginal programs more successful and successful programs more profitable.

What is a logical progression for various direct mail tests? What should you test first? Package? List? Price? Offer? What should you test next?

You could drive yourself crazy developing and assigning priorities for testing. In the process, you could develop one of two afflictions:

Testiphobia (irrational fear of testing)
Testmania (irrational love of testing)

Testiphobia will prevent you from testing. That's not good. Testmania will cause you to become test happy. That's not good either. Either affliction diminishes your chance of success.

To simplify your testing decision, here's a step-by-step checklist. I don't claim that it's the answer for all mailers, but it's reasonable enough that you could follow it without undue concern.

Test #1 - Test Mailing Lists

Create a direct mail package (or have one created) that you feel has the best shot at success. Use it as your initial control package to test various lists of businesses or consumers, recommended by a list broker. Each package sent to each list of prospects or customers (or list segment) must be identified.

Test #2 - Test Package

Create an entirely different package from your control. Change the copy, theme, format and offer. Then take your most responsive lists and use them to test this new package against your control. The winner of this test becomes your control. (Test one and two can be combined using grid testing.)

Test #3 - Test Price

If you have price flexibility, take your control package and change only the price. Nothing else. You might even test three different prices in a three-way test. The price package which wins (using whatever criteria you choose) becomes your control.

Test #4 - Test Offer

Change the offer only. Nothing else (of course, you have to change some of the copy to reflect the change in offer. but only change the copy directly relating to the offer.) You might test a free bonus vs. no bonus, two bonuses vs. one bonus, different bonuses, soft offer vs. hard offer, half-price vs. two-for-one, etc.

Test #5 - Test Copy

Not selected words, but the entire copy thrust. In copy tests, it's usually best to change the primary appeals. You can test copy of individual components like the sales letter, brochure or order form, or everything. All other aspects of the package must remain the same. Do not change offers, colors, formats, paper, etc.

Test #6 - Test Format

On format tests, focus on major changes, not minor ones. For instance, standard envelope mailing vs. a self-mailer, 9 x 12 package vs. a #10 package, personalized vs. non-personalized, (full color vs. one color), etc. Do not change copy thrust or offer.

Keep in mind that 60-70 % of direct marketing success is finding the right audience.

Make an Offer that Cannot Be Refused.

Once you've defined your marketing, you want to come up with an offer that will intrigue the prospect enough so that they will react in a positive fashion. Offers usually contain words like "Free" or "Money-Back If You're Not Satisfied," or "Guaranteed to...," or "For a limited tine only," etc.

Sell Benefits, Not Attributes.

Don't tell what your product is made of or how many pieces of equipment you have in your plant. Tell them what it will do for them. Will it make me happier, richer, more attractive, healthier, etc.? Use words that are easily understandable in a legible format. Fancy graphics are nice, but don't let graphics overwhelm your basic message. On the other hand, strong graphics can help capture attention.

Current Customers are Your Best Customers

You will expend a lot more resources going after new customers with products they have never purchased versus retaining existing customers.

Mailing lists and offers are the two real biggies. They can make a huge difference. Don't sweat the small stuff like color, paperweight, and teaser copy or envelope size.

It's meaningless if you don't track responses and profits. If you don't code your various tests so you track response/profits there's no sense in testing. You must be able to track and analyze tests so that you know what's actually working and what isn't.

How many responses are needed to make a test statistically valid? For a test to be statistically valid (meaning you can have confidence that the results you achieved on the test are likely to occur again when you mail again), you should have a minimum of 30 responses. The more responses you get, the more confident you can be.

Don't rollout to a big list without a retest. Let's say you tested package B against your control package A and B knocked the socks off it. Your inclination is to jump back in with both feet and mail the tail off of B. But before throwing caution to the wind, do a retest. Make sure the results and analysis were accurate. Rule of thumb. Don't mail more than ten times your test quantity on a retest, just in case the initial results were flawed. So, if you tested 5,000 names, retest up to 50,000.

To play it safe, you can use a 75%/25% split. Because they know what to expect (profits) with the control package, many mailers opt not to test because they don't want to give up those known profits. Of course, by not testing they may be missing out on even more profits. There's a solution to this conflict. Instead of testing on a 50-50 basis, you can test at 75%-25% or 80%-20%. You'd mail your control to 75% of the list and the test package to 25% of the list. That way there is little "known" profit risk, but you still get to test. Remember though, for statistical validity, you need 30+ responses.

Some Guidelines

Use the same quantity of names for every list you test. Often this means 5,000 names, since many list owners will not rent smaller quantities for a test.

However, if your budget limits you to testing only one or two similar lists, select the larger list - because they have the most rollout potential. Always test the "hotline" names - the most recent segments of any list - first. If they don't work, no other segment will.

Test new lists early. New lists tend to deliver the highest response rates when they are first placed on the market.

Remailing the same offer to the same audience repeatedly over time will result in a decrease in response.

The smaller the target market, the faster the response will drop off. Varying the package or offer significantly with each new mailing is required to stimulate interest and response.

Use your own customer file to profile against prospecting lists. Segments that have the greatest match are most likely to produce the best response.

Test new products and offers against the most responsive segment of a list.

Every response device should bring back the label or inkjet address or email address from the list including a source code and date stamp. The source code tells you which list generated the reply. The date stamp tells you how long the name has been on the file and its lifetime value since being added to the file.

Customer lists, even when fatigued, tent to outperform prospect files. Therefore, even the oldest segments on your house file should be mailed as long as they produce more orders than the best prospect list.

Never throw away your inactive customer files. Hold them. Lists of inactive customers - even 5 to 9 years old often produce greater response than prospect lists.

It's always better to mail a different segment of the same list, rather than make a repeat mailing to a segment already mailed.

If a list generates a good response, remailing the same promotion to it approximately 8 weeks after the first drop will generate approximately 50 percent of the original response. Example: If the first mailing pulled 5 percent, the second drop will produce around 2.5 percent.

No matter how often you mail to your house file, it is fairly certain you are not mailing enough. If you mail to your house file four times a year, try six or eight times.

Don't test too many variables. If you do, you'll wind up with results anyone can argue with. Remember, you can increase your return on investment by increasing response rates or by decreasing production costs.

Adding an insert will increase your product costs. However, if an insert is appropriate for your mailing and if it is executed properly, it could increase your response rate (and return on investment).

Conclusions

People must be randomly assigned between the various test and control groups. Random samples ensure valid samples across lists, demographics, geography, etc.

Test and control groups must be representative of the population plan to approach in their rollout.

Test and control groups must be treated identically outside of the factor(s) being tested. If not, it will be impossible to interpret and apply results.

Set decision criteria before starting the test and determine the direction you will take based on the decision.

A statistical test will tell you if results are different, but not whether those differences are important

Testing is like proper exercise and diet; it will only provide a benefit if used properly over a long period of time...a little bit of testing will only help very little.

Earlier we said that "Test" is a four-letter word. But so is "Cash".

For more information about testing and list rental I recommend contacting Cindy Dunhill International List Co., Inc. Her e-mail is cindy@dunhills.com .

Appendix 3

A 15-Point Checklist for Your Ad

This article and the article below *Increasing Response Rates of Ads and Direct mail through Imaginative Booklets* by Jeffrey Dobkin are reproduced with permission. If you would like more information contact Mr. Dobkin at Danielle Adams Publishing Co at: 1-610-642-1000.

1. Does it follow the "Five-Second Rule"?
Can readers immediately figure out what you're selling? You really have only three seconds - because it takes two seconds to turn the page and they will. Busy readers won't struggle to figure out your pitch. The Rule: You have a total of five seconds to show them - clearly - what you're selling.

2. Does the headline make them read the rest of the ad?

The sole purpose of the headline is to drive the reader to read the rest of the ad. This is not the place for a sales pitch, this is the place for creating a strong attention-getting, interest-arousing, kick-you-in-the-butt, you-just-gotta-read-the-rest lead-in. Use the Jeff Dobkin 100 to 1 Rule: Write 100 headlines, go back and pick out your best one!

3. Does it have an interest-arousing sub-head?

All ads - space permitting - should have a sub-head. Sub-heads, in slightly-smaller-than-the-headline type, are the transition between the headline and the body copy. This line also doesn't sell the product - its only function is to further interest, hook the reader, and drive him to the body copy.

4. Make sure the first line of the body copy doesn't sell anything, either.

The purpose of this line is still to keep the reader reading - that's its only function. You haven't really hooked the reader until he passes this line, after which he has committed himself to read the rest of the ad IF it's well written. Hence:

5. Do you make a smooth transition from the interest-arousing headline to the sub-

Copyright Clipeze Worldwide, Inc.
Page 196

head to the first line of the body copy which introduces the selling copy in the body of the ad?

This is the last crucial step in making sure your reader continues to read the rest of the ad. In the body copy, you start to sell the response you'd like - usually to make the phone ring.

6. Is your offer clear?

Along with knowing what your product is, if you are selling directly from the ad, do readers know how much it is, and how and where they can purchase it? Don't forget - let them know if it's available directly from you -- and give a big phone number.

7. Does your ad make them want to buy your product?

Does your copy make it sound like it's the best product in the world - one that will get the job done promptly - at the right price? You've got to make your product sound good enough to stop them from going over to Sears and buying it there. It's a tough assignment for a few scribbles on a sheet of paper.

8. Does it make the reader want to rush to the phone to place an order or call for more info?

No, it's not enough to just say it's for sale!
You've got to coerce the reader into action.
Remember, you're working against reader
inertia: a body at rest tends to stay at rest.

9. Does your ad show immediate benefits to the reader?

A product has features, but it's the benefits the
reader gets from the features that make him
buy the product. No one buys a fishing pole
because it's made out of fiberglass - that's a
feature. People buy fishing poles to catch more
fish - a benefit. See?

10. If you have room, can you show several benefits in a bulleted list?

Bulleted lists are easy to see and encourage fly-
by readership. I like to offer three or four of our
biggest benefits in this bulleted form.

11. Did you draft your entire ad to fulfill your ad objective?

If your ad works perfectly as planned, what do
you want people to do? If your objective is lead
generation, your ad will ask the reader to call
(write, or come in) and inquire.

This ad doesn't sell the product, but sells the
response you are requesting. In this case you
say, "Just call and get" and offer a free

informational booklet relating to your product or service. Or "Send for our FREE" Give readers a reason to call. This is a two-step selling approach: the reader calls and gets your hard-hitting sales package, then purchases the product.

With this two-step sale in mind, the entire ad is drafted around generating a call. 90% of the ads I create use this two-step sales formula. If your objective is a direct sale - a one-step selling procedure that sells a product right from the page - it's one of the toughest sales assignments you can give any copywriter.

It's very difficult. But it can be done with a longer-copy ad.

With this direct-sell in mind, the entire ad must be drafted around getting a call and selling the product. It's very difficult and I don't recommend it. It's much easier just to make the phone ring with an inquiry - then YOU sell the product on the phone when they call.

12. Is your guarantee visible?
If you are selling your product directly from the page, make sure your guarantee stands out. I put most guarantees in a small box with a graphic flourish on the top.

13. Is your phone number apparent from three feet away?

If the objective is to have the reader call - and it is in 95% of the ads I create for my clients - I make the phone number easy to see and readily apparent to someone standing looking at the magazine while it is laying on a desk.

14. Is your logo small enough?

That's right, small enough. Unless you run ads in just about every issue of the publication, your logo doesn't need to be large - it's not a selling feature and won't increase your sales or inquiries.

If you do run ads consistently, it's OK to bump it up a notch or two, to about the same size as your phone number. Any bigger while it may massage your ego - just wastes valuable selling space.

15. If it's a direct selling ad, do you have a dashed box around your order coupon?

Why keep readers guessing? Anyone who sees a dashed box knows they can order right from the ad. Some readers need less convincing than others - when they're ready to order a dashed box lets them know right where to go.

Said box also lets browsing readers know that there is an offer and a price to be found in the ad - and this fact will attract even more readers, especially mail order shoppers. These good folks like to order through the mail. Encourage them from their first glance at your ad with this striking graphic.

Increasing Response Rates of Ads and Direct Mail Through Imaginative Booklet Titles. There comes a time in every ad where the reader must respond or the ad fails.

The response to an ad can come in the form of a phone call, a written request, magazine lead sheets—where the reader circles the number on a reader service card or "bingo card"—or the reader comes into the advertiser's retail establishment. But, most likely, it's a phone call.

To create reader movement, the ad must overcome the powerful law of reader inertia: a body at rest tends to stay at rest. There must be an overpowering, driving force to compel the reader into action. The easiest way to accomplish this is to offer something free.

My favorite way of encouraging reader response is to offer a free booklet. Booklets are cheap to produce and can be directed at a specific want or need. OK, so a free booklet isn't the Cartier watch your readers thought they were going to get when they noticed the word FREE in the ad. But the word "FREE" (remember to always set in caps - to make it stand out from the rest of the line and get better readership, 'eye candy' I call it) gets the attention of even the stingiest of readers, then the booklet title makes them pick up the phone and gives readers a reason to call. The better the title, the stronger the reason and the drive to call.

Asking readers to call for a free booklet is what I refer to as a "non-threatening reason to call." For readers with any fear of the telephone, for people who don't know what to say when they pick up the phone to call a stranger, for the intimidated who think death is better than getting a salesperson on the phone who may try to sell them something, being able to ask for a free booklet is manna from heaven - and one of the best ways to maximize call-in response. "Oh, I'll just call them and ask for this FREE booklet!" And here's the huge benefit for you: response by telephone is the easiest way for advertisers to instantly get additional information about their audience.

When someone calls me and asks for a free booklet, the last thing I do is get his name and address so that I can send him a free booklet. That's the last thing I do. The first thing I do is ask a few quick, prying and fiendishly-penetrating questions, so that I can qualify him as a suspect, a prospect, or someone with a phone next to his desk and a few moments of free time while waiting for his lunch to arrive.

Ask callers probing questions, such as "Oh, were you in the market for one of these?" "When were you thinking of buying one?" and "What color did you like the best?" When people are getting something for free they're generally more than willing to answer a few questions." They wouldn't want to jeopardize their free gift by not responding to your brief interview, would they? Since they're getting something free, they're usually in a happy and receptive mood. After all, they're getting something for FREE.

The real value of offering a free booklet is to make your phone ring. When your phone rings, the ad worked. Period. It's not the job of the ad to sell anything - the sole job of the ad was to make the phone ring. Yes, it's all over for the ad - it did all you asked it to, and its objective is now completely fulfilled. When the phone rang, its mission was accomplished. The ad can do no more. It's your turn now.

The ball is back in your court to figure out how to turn the person on the phone into a buyer. Over the years, I've had many clients who have said, "Yes, the phone was ringing off the hook, but the ad was a failure - not one person bought anything." If the phone was ringing off the hook, the ad worked. The problem was somewhere else in the marketing program. But that's another article.

Offering Booklets Instead of Brochures
If you said in your ad you're giving away a brochure, people think, "so what - everybody gives away their brochure." It's true - just go into any car dealership and if you have a wood burning stove you can come home with enough brochures to keep your house heated for an Alaskan winter.

With a little bit of forethought you can transform your brochure into an informative booklet. At worst, design your brochure to fold in half - making an 8-1/2" x 11" sheet into a 5 1/2" x 8 1/2" four pager you can safely call a "booklet." For additional credibility, add one more sheet folded the same way and nested inside. Now, you definitely do have a booklet.

Creating "Drive-Them-Nuts" Content

The drive to make readers call can come from 2 directions: pitching content or title. Both are similar - your assignment is to create the most compelling set of words to make the reader call. It sounds so simple, doesn't it?

When creating content for your literature, can you think of 10 questions that everyone in your market will drive 40 miles to get the answers to? Write them down, and then use the top 3 or 4 in your ad. I'm talking questions so penetrating that if the reader throws out the magazine, he'll wake up in the middle of the night, go downstairs and dig it out of the trash so he can call you first thing in the morning to get your booklet. Now, that's the kind of burning questions we're looking for.

Examples of questions: "Find out 3 ways to get home with an 8-foot table and a 6-foot car trunk. Call now for our FREE Booklet on Car Tricks" Our FREE Booklet also includes "Flat tire and no spare? How to get home safely." Plus, "The four ways gas stations cheat almost every customer at the pump - and how to avoid them!"

Stop Them Cold with a Promise or an "I-Can't-Believe-It" Title

The best way to make the phone ring is to paralyze people with the title of a booklet that sounds so good they can't possibly pass it up. It's the title of the booklet that drives the reader crazy and makes sure he calls. A promise of information so outstanding the reader just has to know it. "What to do: Flat tire and no spare? Call for our free booklet 'How to get home quickly and safely.' It's FREE!" There is only one rule: your booklet title has to be great enough to make the phone ring consistently. Nope, not just "good" - it has to be great.

Using Titles to Limit Response to More Qualified Prospects

Tired of sending literature to everyone, and their mothers? Booklet titles can almost hand pick which readers will respond, thereby setting thresholds of prospect qualifications. The booklet title can throw a loose or tight qualification net, whatever you like, or whatever the product calls for. If your product is widely used, has good margins, and your literature is a hard-hitting direct mail piece that pulls a 25% response, throw a loose net and invite everyone to call. Raise the bar if your product has low margins, your literature is expensive and your market limited to a few at the top.

An offer for a free booklet on how to install a new roof is only of interest to people needing new roofs. So is a FREE booklet on "6 Major Considerations before You Buy a New Roof!" or

"Selecting, Grading and Pricing a Shingle Roof for Your Home." Voila - instant qualification.

When the phone rings, the caller is looking for a new roof. A FREE booklet on how to pack valuables for moving? You guessed it - this free booklet is fascinating, but only to people thinking about moving. Save on literature costs by restricting your marketing message to the really interested, and your most likely purchasing candidates.

By the way - see the difference in reading: I've used the word FREE in this last paragraph four times, two in all capital letters and two in lower case. Notice how differently they are read? The "FREE" in capitals yells at you - it commands attention and makes you stop and notice it. The "free" in lower case blends into the rest of the copy and lets you continue to read without even a pause.

A Simple Way to Create Great Booklet Titles

The question finally arises, "Jeff, how do I consistently think up these compelling booklet titles?" You're not going to like this: you follow the Jeff Dobkin hundred-to-one rule: "Write 100 titles, then go back and pick out your best one." Yep. Same with intriguing questions about the content: write 100 questions, go back and pick out your best 3. Hey, I didn't say it would be easy, I just said it would be simple. It's simple and effective.

Yes, it's a little more work writing 100 titles, but the real question is this: Do you want the absolute best return on your advertising dollar? Is the objective of your ad to compel the most people you possibly can to pick up the phone and call? Offering a FREE booklet can do just that. And it's cheaper to spend the extra hour or two writing a better booklet title than placing ads and getting only half the response you could be receiving. Isn't it? Again you can see more tips on Jeff's site at www.Dobkin.com

Forms

The following forms are for illustration to help you understand dealing with vendors and customers in the operation of your business.

Laws vary from state to state and it is advised to consult an attorney in your state before using them.

Mutual Nondisclosure Agreement

This agreement is made effective on _____ (date) by and between _____ (first party) and _____ (second party) (collectively, the "Parties"), to ensure the protection and preservation of the confidential and/or proprietary nature of information disclosed or made available or to be disclosed or made available to each other. For the purposes of this agreement, each Party shall be deemed to include any subsidiaries, internal divisions, agents, and employees. Any signing party shall refer to and bind the individual and the entity that he or she represents.

Whereas the Parties desire to ensure the confidential status of the information that may be disclosed to each other.

Now, therefore, in reliance upon and in consideration of the following undertakings, the Parties agree as follows:

1. Subject to limitations set forth in paragraph 2, all information disclosed to the other party shall be deemed to be "Proprietary Information." In particular, Proprietary Information shall be deemed to include any information, marketing technique, publicity technique, public relations technique, process, technique, algorithm, program, design, drawing, mask work, formula, test data research project, work in progress, future development, engineering, manufacturing, marketing, servicing, financing or personal matter relating to the disclosing party, its present or future products, sales, suppliers, clients, customers, employees, investors or business, whether in oral, written, graphic or electronic form.

2. The term "Proprietary Information" shall not be deemed to include information that (i) is now, or hereafter becomes, through no act or failure to act on the part of the receiving party, generally known or available information, (ii) is known by the receiving party at the time of receiving such information as evidenced by its records, (iii) is hereafter furnished to the receiving party by a

third party, as a matter of right and without restriction on disclosure, (iv) is independently developed by the receiving party without reference to the information disclosed hereunder, or (v) is the subject of a written permission to disclose provided by the disclosing party.

Not withstanding any other provision of this Agreement, disclosure of Proprietary Information shall not be precluded if such disclosure:

a. Is in response to a valid order of a court or other governmental body of the United States or any political subdivision thereof,

b. Is otherwise required by law, or,

c. Is otherwise necessary to establish rights or enforce obligations under this agreement, but only to the extent that any such disclosure is necessary.

In the event that the receiving party is requested in any proceedings before a court or any other governmental body to disclose proprietary information, it shall give the disclosing party prompt notice of such request so that the disclosing party may seek an appropriate protective order. If, in the absence of a protective order, the receiving party is nonetheless compelled to disclose proprietary information, the receiving party may disclose such information without liability hereunder, provided, however, that such party gives the disclosing party advance written notice of the information to be disclosed and, upon the request and at the expense of the disclosing party, uses its best efforts to obtain assurances that confidential treatment will be accorded to such information.

Each party shall maintain in trust and confidence and not disclose to any third party or use for any unauthorized purpose any proprietary information received from the other party. Each party may use such proprietary information in the extent required to accomplish the purpose of the discussions with respect to the subject. Proprietary Information shall not be used for any purpose or in any manner that would constitute a violation on law regulations, including without limitation the export control laws of the United States of America. No other rights or licenses to trademarks, inventions, copyrights or patents are implied or granted under this Agreement.

Proprietary information supplied shall not be reproduced in any form except as required to accomplish the intent of this Agreement.

The responsibilities of the Parties are limited to using their efforts to protect the Proprietary Information received with the same degree of care used to protect their own Proprietary

Information from unauthorized use or disclosure. Both Parties shall advise their employees or agents who might have access to such Proprietary Information of the confidential nature thereof and that by receiving such information they are agreeing to be bound by this Agreement. No Proprietary Information shall be disclosed to any officer, employee, or agent of either party who does not have a need for such information for the purpose of the discussions with respect to the subject.

All Proprietary Information (including all copies thereof) shall remain the property of the disclosing party and shall be returned to the disclosing party after the receiving party's need for it has expired, or upon request of the disclosing party, and in any event, upon completion or termination of this Agreement. The receiving party further agrees to destroy all notes and copies thereof made by its officers and employees containing or based on any Proprietary Information and to cause all agents and representatives to whom or to which Proprietary Information has been disclosed to destroy all notes and copies in their possession that contain Proprietary Information.

This Agreement shall survive any termination of the discussion with respect to the subject and shall continue in full force and effect until such time as Parties mutually agree to terminate it.

This Agreement shall be governed by the laws of the United States of America and as those laws that are applied to contracts entered into and to be performed in all states. Should any revision of this Agreement be determined to be void, invalid or otherwise unenforceable by any court or tribunal of competent jurisdiction, such determination shall not affect the remaining provisions of this Agreement, which shall remain in full force and effect.

This Agreement contains final, complete, and exclusive agreement of the Parties relative to the subject matter hereof and supersedes any prior agreement of the Parties, whether oral or written. This Agreement may not be changed, modified, amended or supplemented except by a written instrument signed by both Parties.

Each party hereby acknowledges and agrees that, in the event of any breach of this Agreement by the other party, including, without limitations, the actual or threatened disclosure of a disclosing party's Proprietary Information without the prior express written consent of the disclosing party, the disclosing party will suffer an irreparable injury such that no remedy at law will afford it adequate protection against or appropriate compensation for such injury. Accordingly, each party hereby agrees that the other party shall be entitled to specific performance of a receiving party's obligations under this Agreement as well as further injunctive relief as may be granted by a court of competent jurisdiction.

The term of this agreement is for two (2) years, commencing on the "Effective Date."

AGREED TO:

Signature

_____

Printed Name

_____

Date: _____

AGREED TO:

Signature

_____

Printed Name

_____

Date: _____

Purchase Order

[Company Name]

[Company Slogan]

PURCHASE ORDER

DATE:	4/19/2008
P.O. #	[123456]
Customer	[123]

[Street Address]
[City, ST ZIP]
Phone: [000-000-0000]
Fax: [000-000-0000]

VENDOR

[Name]
[Company Name]
[Street Address]
[City, ST ZIP]
[Phone]

SHIP TO

[Attn: Name]
[Company Name]
[Street Address]
[City, ST ZIP]
[Phone]

REQUISITIONE	SHIP VIA	F.O.B.	SHIPPING TERMS

ITEM #	DESCRIPTION	QTY	UNIT PRICE	TOTAL
[23423423]	Product XYZ	15	150.00	2,250.00
[45645645]	Product ABC	1	75.00	75.00
				-
				-
				-
				-
				-
				-
				-
				-
				-

Other Comments or Special Instructions

SUBTOTAL	$	2,325.00
TAX RATE		6.875%
TAX	$	159.84
S & H	$	-
OTHER	$	-
TOTAL	**$**	**2,484.84**

_____   _____
Authorized by   Date

If you have any questions about this purchase order, please contact
[Name, Phone #, E-mail, Phone, Fax]

Invoice

[Company Name]

[Company Slogan]
[web address]

[Street Address]
[City, ST ZIP]
Phone: [000-000-0000]
Fax: [000-000-0000]

INVOICE

DATE:	4/19/2008
INVOICE #	[123456]
Customer	[123]

BILL TO:

[Name]
[Company Name]
[Street Address]
[City, ST ZIP]
[Phone]

SHIP TO (if different):

[Name]
[Company Name]
[Street Address]
[City, ST ZIP]
[Phone]

SALESPERSON	P.O. #	SHIP DATE	SHIP VIA	F.O.B.	TERMS

ITEM #	DESCRIPTION	QTY	UNIT PRICE	TOTAL
[23423423]	Product XYZ	15	150.00	2,250.00
[45645645]	Product ABC	1	75.00	75.00
				-
				-
				-
				-
				-
				-
				-
				-
				-
				-

Other Comments or Special Instructions

1. Total payment due in 30 days
2. Please include the invoice number on your check

SUBTOTAL	$	2,325.00
TAX RATE		6.875%
TAX	$	159.84
S & H	$	-
OTHER	$	-
TOTAL		######

Make all checks payable to
[Your Company Name]

If you have any questions about this invoice, please contact
[Name, Phone #, E-mail]
Thank You For Your Business!

Sales Representative Agreement

THIS AGREEMENT by and between, whose addresses are,
hereinafter referred to as "Company", and
, whose address is
, hereinafter referred to as "Sales Representative".

WHEREAS, Company is engaged in the marketing and sale of   ; and

WHEREAS, Sales Representative desires to sell Company's services in
accordance with the terms and conditions of this Agreement.

NOW, THEREFORE, it is agreed as follows:
1. Company hereby appoints Sales Representative as an authorized non-exclusive independent representative to sell and promote all services
provided by Company in the following geographical area:_____
hereinafter referred to as "Territory".

2. Sales Representative shall devote such time, energy and skill on a
regular and consistent basis as is necessary to sell and promote the sale

of Company's services in the Territory during
the term of this Agreement.
Sales Representative's sales and promotional
efforts shall be directed
toward the following_____ .

The aforementioned customers are intended
only to be examples of the nature and type of
market to which Company desires that its
services be sold and should not be construed as
a limitation upon the contracts that can be
made
by Sales Representative under this Agreement
within the designated market. In addition to
the foregoing, Sales Representative shall assist
Company and shall perform any and all services
required or requested in connection with
Company's business , including, but not limited
to, such services of an advisory nature as may
be requested from time to time by Company.

Sales Representative shall periodically, or at
any time upon Company's request, submit
appropriate documentation of any and all sales
and promotional
efforts performed and to be performed for
Company pursuant to this Agreement.

3. For each contract for the performance of
Company's services as arranged

by Sales Representative under this Agreement, Sales Representative shall be
entitled to a commission as follows:
a. (%) percent of contract billing during the first year; b. (%)
percent of contract billing during the second year; c. (%) percent of
contract billing during the third year, and for any year thereafter.
The commission rates and time periods set forth in this paragraph shall commence as of the date of the first invoice on the contract; provided, however that no commission will be due and payable to Sales Representative
until   ( ) days from receipt of payment of Company from any
customer on the contract for any underlying invoice. Commissions will be paid on fees for services rendered by shall not include freight, supplies, and other charges incidental to the performance of said services.

For purposes of this Agreement, "Contract" shall mean any agreement and/or order of Company's services sold or arranged by Sales Representative. Any and all commissions payable to Company to Sales Representative under this
Agreement shall terminate on the   day of the full month after termination of this Agreement

and Company shall then be discharged and released of any further obligation to pay commissions to Sales Representative under this Agreement.

4. During the term of this Agreement or within year(s) after its termination, Sales Representative, or any agents or representatives under Sales Representative's control, shall not compete with Company, directly or indirectly, for Sales Representative or on behalf of any other person, firm, partnership, corporation or other entity in the sale or promotion of services the same as or similar to Company's services within the Territory. Under no circumstances and at no time shall Sales Representative disclose to any person any of the secrets, methods or systems used by Company in its business. All customer lists, brochures, reports, and other such information of any nature made available to Sales Representative by virtue of Sales Representative's association with Company shall be held in strict confidence during the term of this Agreement and after its termination.

5. This Agreement shall not create a partnership, joint venture, agency, employer/employee or similar relationship

between Company and Sales Representative. Sales Representative shall be an independent contractor.
Company shall not be required to withhold any amounts for state or federal income tax or for FICA taxes from sums becoming due to Sales Representative under this Agreement. Sales Representative shall not be considered an employee of Company and shall not be entitled to participate in any plan,
Arrangement or distribution by Company pertaining to or in connection with any pension, stock, bonus, profit sharing or other benefit extended to Company's employees. Sales Representative shall be free to utilize his time, energy and skill in such manner, as he deems advisable to the extent
that he is not otherwise obligated under this Agreement.

6. Sales Representative shall bear any and all costs or expenses incurred by Sales Representative to perform his obligation under this Agreement, including, but not limited to, vehicle insurance, travel expenses and telephone expenses.

7. The rights and duties of Sales Representative under this Agreement are personal and may not

be assigned or delegated without prior written consent of Company.

8. Sales Representative is not authorized to extend any warranty or guarantee or to make representations or claims with respect to Company's services without express written authorization from Company.

9. Sales Representative shall indemnify and hold Company harmless of and from any and all claims or liability arising as a result of negligent, intentional or other acts of Sales Representative or his agent or representatives.

10. Company shall indemnify and hold Sales Representative harmless of and from any and all liability attributable solely to the negligent, intentional or other acts of Company or its employees.

11. This agreement, and all transactions contemplated hereby, shall be governed by, construed and enforced in accordance with the laws of the State of. The Parties herein waive trial by jury and agree to submit to the personal jurisdiction and venue of a court of subject matter jurisdiction located in   County, State of . In the event that litigation results from or arises out of this Agreement or the

performance thereof, the Parties agree to reimburse the prevailing party's reasonable attorney's fees, court costs, and all other expenses, whether or not taxable by the court as costs, in addition to any other relief to which the prevailing party may be entitled. In such event, no action shall be entertained by said court or any court of competent jurisdiction if filed more than one year subsequent to the date the cause(s) of action actually accrued regardless of whether damages were otherwise as of said time calculable.

12. Any notice under this Agreement shall be deemed given on the third
business day following the mailing of any such notice, postage paid, to the address set forth above.
13. This Agreement contains the entire agreement between the parties and
any representation, promise or condition not incorporated herein shall not be binding upon either party.

IN WITNESS WHEREOF, the parties have hereunto executed this Agreement on
the   day of   , 20 , to become effective as of
, 20 .

"COMPANY"

By:
Witness   President

Witness

Witness

"SALES REPRESENTATIVE "Witness

References

Books and publications

*How to Market a Product For Under
$500* and *Uncommon Marketing Techniques*
by Jeffrey Dobkin
The Danielle Adams Publishing Company
http://www.dobkin.com/

These two books are the best marketing books I
have ever found. In my opinion Jeffrey Dobkin
is the best direct marketer in the country. I keep
his books on my desk and I reread them at least
once a year. I followed his books to the letter
when I started my business. I can truly say that
his marketing systems work. He has a unique
blend of humor and frankness in his writing
style. Jeff also consults with small businesses
and I can attest to his ability and honesty.

Patent it Yourself
 by David Pressman,
Nolo Publishing Company
http://www.nolo.com/

Mr. Pressman is a patent attorney with vast knowledge of the patent process. He gives his readers step-by-step instructions for filing a patent application.

Rich Dad Poor Dad Series
by Robert Kiyosaki,
Warner Business Books Publishing Company
http://www.twbookmark.com
www.richdad.com

Guerrilla Marketing for the Home Based Business
by Jay Levinson and Seth Godin
Houghton Mifflin Company.

The Guerrilla Marketing Handbook
Trade Show Marketing
Guerrilla Negotiating
by The Guerrilla Group Inc
http://www.guerrillagroup.com

Negotiation for Dummies
by Michael C. Donaldson and Mimi Donaldson
IDG Books
http://www.dummies.com/

80/20 Principle
by Richard Koch
www.bdd.com

Customers for Keeps: 8 Powerful Strategies to Turn Customers into Friends and Keep Them Forever
Sold! Direct Marketing
Response! The Complete Guide to Profitable Direct Marketing
By Lois K. Geller
http://www.amazon.com/
http://www.loisgellermarketinggroup.com/

The Inventor's Desktop Companion
by Richard C. Levy
http://www.amazon.com/

Resources found on the Internet

US Patent and Trademark Office
http://www.uspto.gov/

Legal Information
Nolo Publishing
800-992-6656
www.nolo.com .

Google.com Search Engine
http://www.google.com/

Clipart.com for logo and brochures and catalogs
http://www.clipart.com/

Clipart.com is the best web site I have found for royalty free clip art for your use. They have over 10-million downloadable images. Subscriptions are available for a week, month, three months, six months, and one year or for two years. Prices start as low as $14.95.

Wikipedia
http://en.wikipedia.org/

A wonderful, free encyclopedia. If you do not understand a business term or want to find out more information about a certain subject the place to start is Wikipedia. Everyone should bookmark this web address for fast access.

DUNHILL LIST CO., INC.
http://www.dunhills.com

Cindy Dunhill is very knowledgeable and will help you with your lit rental needs

Sources for finding manufacturers in Asia
Taiwan Commerce Directory
http://www.commerce.com.tw

http://globalsources.com/

http://alibaba.com/

Directories that can be purchased or are found at your local college library:

The National Directory of Mail Order Catalogs
By Gray House Publishing
http://www.greyhouse.com/

Thomas Directory
Manufacturers and business in any given industry.
http://www.thomasnet.com/

Bacon's Newspaper and Magazine Guide
 For press releases and ads
Bacon's Information Inc
800-621-0561
www.baconsinfo.com

Order Securely On-line at:
http://www.garybronga.com

For orders by postal mail:
Send a check for $19.99 plus $6.99 shipping and
handling
(Total $26.98)
to
Clipeze Worldwide Inc.,
PO Box 373
Mims, FL 32754-0373

Make checks payable to CLIPEZE Worldwide
Inc. For telephone credit card orders call
800-385-0014
The retail price of this book is $19.99

Call for discount rates for volume sales.

Gary R. Bronga is available for speaking to your
group or association. Buying this book entitles
you to a discount for the unlimited consultations
with Gary by phone program. Call for details.

Call toll fee 1-800-384-0014

Promote YOUR Business with this Book

1. Send this book to clients at the year-end holiday or any other time, thanking them for their business.

2. Use the book as a thank-you for a sales appointment.

3. Mail a book to prospects to stay in touch with them.

4. Offer the book free with purchase in a specific time, for certain purchase amount, or opening an account.

5. Distribute this book to prospects at a trade show.

6. Give the book as an incentive for completing a questionnaire or survey or for helping purge a mailing list.

7. Include a book in a mailing of invoices as a thank you.

8. Package a book with a product as a value-added.

9. Deliver a copy of the book to the first x number of people to enter a drawing or come to a store.

10. Provide copies of a book to people and organizations that can refer business to you.

Made in the USA
San Bernardino, CA
26 December 2013